pork

PORK

More than 50 Heavenly Meals that Celebrate
the Glory of Pig, Delicious Pig

Cree LeFavour
Photographs by Antonis Achilleos

CHRONICLE BOOKS
SAN FRANCISCO

Designed by
— SARA SCHNEIDER —

10 9 8 7 6 5 4 3 2 1

— CHRONICLE BOOKS LLC —
680 SECOND STREET
SAN FRANCISCO, CALIFORNIA 94107
WWW.CHRONICLEBOOKS.COM

FOR BRUCE LEFAVOUR
AND FAITH ECHTERMEYER

ACKNOWLEDGMENTS

Major thanks to everyone at Chronicle Books. It's my privilege to work with every one of you. I'm thinking of Lorena Jones, Bill LeBlond (you are missed!), Sarah Billingsley, Amy Treadwell, Deborah Kops, Sara Schneider, David Hawk, Peter Perez, Doug Ogan, Marie Oishi, and Steve Kim. Particular thanks go to you, Sarah, for your sparkling intelligence and steady good sense as an editor. To David McCormick, the most relaxed but sneakily effective agent ever, thanks for making it all happen. Thanks to Antonis Achilleos for having the eye to capture the look and feel of the food in his photographs and for carrying off the job with such grace and precision. Harold McGee, guru of cooking science, thank you for your research and clarity in your indispensible book *On Food and Cooking*. My copy is happily dog-eared and grease-stained. My gratitude and admiration goes out to three great cooks who keep me inspired and happy to be in the kitchen—Jonny Miles, Shelley Boris, and Jean-Pierre Moullé. For making so many ribs and chops disappear without flinching at the onslaught of more to come, I have Dwight Garner and Penn Garner LeFavour to thank. To Hattie Garner LeFavour, my resident vegetarian, thanks for so cheerfully tolerating a year of pork.

CONTENTS

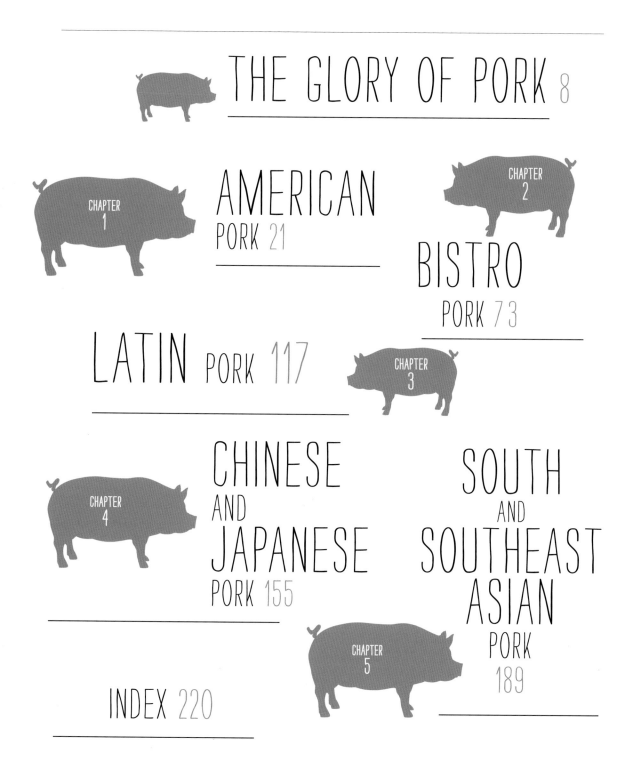

THE GLORY OF PORK

In 1974, the year my family moved to Idaho from Colorado, our two giant pigs, Woody and Aspen, lived in what would become our vegetable garden. We'd named them, nostalgically, after the place we'd come from—Little Woody Creek, in Aspen, where the gonzo writer Hunter S. Thompson was just one of many close neighbors in our tight community. Far away, at our historic ranch, called Robinson Bar, nestled along the Salmon River in central Idaho, the pigs slept in an insulated red doghouse, stuffed with straw. Over the long winter, when the thermometer stuck at -10°F/-23°C for stretches of a week or more, Woody and Aspen burrowed deep in their small house, emerging only when we approached with their bucket of warm, fragrant kitchen slops. Their stout bodies, covered in coarse hair, steamed in the air.

That spring, we shot them and slaughtered them steps from where they were raised. Their dark, richly flavored meat was irresistible, even to me. That was the last time my sister and I named our pigs.

I adore every part of the pig. Not just the big meaty parts like the chops, loin, ham, and shoulder, but also the fatty belly and jowls, the head for headcheese, the tail for frying Laura Ingalls Wilder-style, and the trotters for stock making and gnawing on. Lusty, fatty, juicy—pork is *the* food obsession of the decade.

Ten years ago, unless you raised it yourself, you were stuck with commercial meat—lean, flavorless, and wan. The idea of breeding hogs to be "the other white meat," low in fat and neutral tasting, was never, ever a good one. Today, in all but the smallest grocery stores, if you look for it, you'll discover richly flavored pork that will charm and dazzle you when cooked simply with nothing more than a pinch of salt. Don't be fooled by the word "natural." The meat you want will come from humanely raised, antibiotic-free animals. It might or might not be USDA (U.S. Department of Agriculture)-certified organic (see page 12), but it will be clearly differentiated from the other pork in the store. In better stores and at farmers' markets, you'll find meat from heritage breed pigs selected for flavor, fat, and tenderness. They might not have been raised on slop in the backyard, but you can be sure they've been living something closer to a pig's life, with grain, grass, mud, and room to move about. This is meat worthy of your kitchen.

My goal here is to take on pork in all its glorious variations. In pursuit of this goal, I've created recipes and sides inspired by the pig-eating traditions of the world. I have loosely defined these by region, dividing them into chapters: American, European (the "Bistro" chapter), Latin, Chinese and Japanese, and South and Southeast Asian. As obsession-worthy as simply cooked pork is—and anyone who has tasted slow-cooked pork belly knows that it is—the pig discovers its genius when it bumps up against the walloping flavors that a truly global grab bag of spices, sauces, methods, and aromatics delivers. These piquant flavors, paired with bright, bold side dishes, are the kinds of meals you'll find on every page of *Pork*.

So if you want to throw a bunch of pork chops on the grill to serve with a couple of simple sides on a Wednesday night, I'll show you the way. Then again, if you want to show off at a dinner party but need to be guided and inspired to pull off pork ribs and adzuki beans braised in ginger-, lemongrass-, and anise-scented stock and served over soba noodles, *Pork* is your book. From simple, fast meals for a weeknight dinner to feasts worthy of the most demanding guest, it's all here. I'm committed to fresh, beautiful, brightly flavored food that home cooks can put on the table with relative ease.

Simple dishes can be exceptional if you start with superior ingredients. Pick recipes that inspire you, and stick to seasonal vegetables and fruits, mixing up the sides across recipe sets to make use of the best and freshest produce. Keep high-quality vinegars and olive oils on hand (for more on olive oil, see page 18)—there's no easier way to boost the flavor of a dish than by using a subtle, flavorful vinegar or a spot of fruity, potent olive oil.

Shop with care and pay a little more for your eggs, cream, and butter. Whether you're cooking a dish that's simple or complex, the elements matter. A curry made with two-year-old spices isn't going to taste anything like the curry made with spices you've just bought from a stellar source, just as a carrot slaw made from a bag of dried-out, split carrots packed in

plastic weeks—or months—ago isn't going to match one made with carrots bought fresh, their tops still on. Without occupying your entire existence with the quest for kitchen treasure, grab what you can when you see it, whether it's an oversize bag of fava beans you spot while strolling through the farmers' market or a spectacular (and spectacularly expensive) bottle of Champagne vinegar in a specialty kitchen store. The food you cook and eat at home will radiate with your efforts, reflecting a pronounced step up in flavor, texture, and appearance.

BUYING PORK

The quality of pork you can buy varies vastly. While the cut or location of the meat on the animal is important, other factors are even more critical. First, the breed of a pig will determine how much fat the animal carries, how marbled the meat is, and where it packs on that fat (loin or leg, shoulder or belly). In addition, the breed is a factor in determining the color of the meat and consequently its flavor and texture. Heritage breeds popular with farmers committed to sustainably raising delicious meat include Hampshire, Berkshire, Large Black, Mulefoot, Red Wattle, Tamworth, Mangalitsa, Gloucestershire Old Spot, Guinea, Kurobuta, and Ossabaw. These breeds aren't selected for their lean meat.

Swine raised in what are grimly referred to as concentrated animal feeding operations (CAFOs), more often than not owned by Smithfield Foods, are usually Chester White, American Yorkshire, or sometimes the versatile Duroc. Whatever breed the pig, the animal's diet is the next most crucial factor. What the pig eats—wheat, soy meal, corn, grass, dairy, nuts, fish, or a mess of human slops—has an essential impact on the flavor of the meat.

The meat from organically certified pigs and pigs raised on small farms with access to pasture have a richer, more complex flavor than the meat from pigs that have been kept indoors and fattened on wheat, soy, and corn pig pellets every meal of their short lives. In addition, the walking, running, and rooting about that pigs do when outdoors on pasture determines, along with the breed of pig, how tender the meat will be and how dark in color. (Dark meat on chickens and pigs isn't so different; think of shoulder and ham as dark and the loin as somewhat equivalent to the lighter meat on the breast.) Most important of all, as anyone who has gnawed the fatty meat off a chop bone knows, the quantity of fat in and around the meat has a great deal to do with flavor and texture.

PRIMAL CUTS

When a pig is slaughtered, its carcass is divided into four or five primal cuts or sections: shoulder (or shoulder butt and picnic shoulder), loin, belly, and ham (rear leg). It's pretty confusing trying to figure out which cut to buy when there are so many choices and when the names of the cuts don't always include the name of the primal cut (which should be mentioned somewhere on the package, but often isn't).

SHOULDER BUTT AND PICNIC SHOULDER
This section of the pig from the top of the animal's shoulder to its foot weighs in at around 30 lb/13.6 kg. The top half of the shoulder, often separated into its own subprimal cut as Boston butt, may be sold in large pieces as Boston butt, Boston

shoulder, pork butt, Boston blade roast, or just blade roast—or the take-it-all-in-one as pork shoulder Boston butt blade roast. (I've seen this!) The lower, or leg, portion is often labeled picnic, picnic shoulder, or pork shoulder arm picnic. Below the picnic shoulder are the hock and trotters (pig's feet). Yes, the names can be confusing because butchers from different schools of butchery and regions call these parts by different names, and because the "butt" is actually the shoulder.

The meat that comes from the shoulder as a whole may be cut into seemingly end-less smaller cuts, including country-style ribs, shoulder chops, cubes and kebabs, shoulder blade roast, shoulder blade steak, shoulder arm steak, picnic ham (even though a real ham comes from only the rear leg), and brisket, which is designated as flat or point and may be called boneless shoulder breast. (Yep, a cut called brisket is found on a cow and on a pig, although trust me, don't go calling this section of meat "brisket" in public, or you'll get into all kinds of food fights—unless, that is, your audience really knows their meat.)

THE BELLY
There are about 35 lb/15.9 kg of meat here—the fattiest meat on the animal. Bacon, of course, comes from the belly (it's just smoked and cured pork belly). Sometimes belly is referred to as side, as in fresh side or fresh side boneless half. St. Louis ribs, spareribs, and rib tips come from the belly. St. Louis ribs are spareribs with the irregular tips cut off—hence the rib tips. Meat labeled as "country ribs" may also come from the belly or side of the carcass, but more often they're not ribs at all, coming as they usually do from the front section of the loin or the blade end, next to the shoulder. Argh! Confusing, I know.

THE LOIN

This is the leanest meat and the lightest in color, since loin muscle is used less than others and therefore contains less myoglobin, similar to breast meat on a chicken or turkey. Weighing in around 35 lb/15.9 kg, the meat from the loin is tender but can easily dry out when you cook it because it contains so little fat. Look for all those delicious chops that may be labeled center cut, top loin, butterfly, sirloin chops, rib-eye chops, blade chops, and porterhouse chops. (Sounds like beef, right?)

To simplify the chop taxonomy: There are chops cut from the center of the loin (center cut), from the shoulder end (rib chops), and from the sirloin or back end (end chops). Then there are all the loin cuts that are versions of the above chops, left intact: rib roast (bone in or not, frenched or not), New York roast, sirloin roast, and top loin roast, among others. Don't forget the tenderloin, a very lean cut from the middle of the loin section, at the rear. It takes well to big sauces but doesn't have a whole lot of character on its own—it's also called "filet" or "tenderloin filet." The remaining meat from the loin includes baby back ribs, sirloin cutlets, sirloin cubes, kebab meat, and country ribs. This is not an exhaustive list, but it covers most of what you need to know.

THE HAM

This is the name for both the primal cut and the ubiquitous smoked and cured product we all know so well. The whole cut weighs in at around 45 lb/20.4 kg. To distinguish it from the smoked and cured meat, you'll see it marked fresh ham in the meat case. If the leg has been cut in half, which it often is since the whole ham is so large, you may see "ham shank half, bone in" or "ham shank boneless." Often, you won't see the word "ham" at all—only the word "leg," as in leg eye roast, leg bottom roast, leg top roast, leg tip roast, leg rump roast, and Des Moines roast. Look for ham cut into steaks under the names sliced leg, leg steak, and leg center slice—among others. Don't forget the bottom of the leg, called the shank, which comes in a range of bone-in, sliced, and whole cuts, and, of course, the second pair of trotters.

ODD BITS

These are the tasty parts that you'll need to work a little harder to get from the barnyard to your plate. I'm talking about the ears, snout, neck bones, tail, jowls, skin, and, best of all, the whole head, which you can roast, cook in parts, or braise. Of course there's also headcheese, which requires cooking the head, pulling off and seasoning the meat, and then packing it in a terrine to set with a little extra gelatin. (Just be sure you have a gigantic pot or a razor-sharp saw so you can fit that whole head in a pot!) As for innards, keep your eye out for the heart, tongue, liver, ruffle fat, and caulfat. If you're truly brave, you can seek out brain, testicles, spleen, intestines, and, best of all, the bung (hog bung, pig bung—it's all the same: lower intestine with the rectum attached). There is no shortage of recipes when it comes to these lovely, hard-to-find parts of the animal, whether you've gotten your hands on a fresh liver for making paté or odd bits for making some fabulous Old World meat concoction encased in aspic or caulfat or packed into a terrine. This book will take you as far as the ears, trotters, hocks, and neck for making astonishingly good Ear Gear (page 102) and Rich Stock (page 181).

AT THE SUPERMARKET

In the supermarket meat case, cuts from the pig's loin—pork chops, tenderloin, and loin roasts—dominate. In addition to those, you'll also see big, irregular hunks of meat: Boston butt, shoulder roast, shoulder, picnic ham, rib chops, and fresh ham. Conventional wisdom and most cookbooks will tell you that the big hunks are strictly for slow cooking and braising because they're tough, while cuts from the loin are tender and should not be over-cooked. This is partly true—you should not overcook any meat from the loin. But many cooks assume, incorrectly, that the meat from the shoulder and ham are too tough to panfry or grill as they might a pork chop. Actually, the meat from these sections is more flavorful and fattier (fat equals flavor!) than the meat from the sometimes pallid loin section.

What I suggest as you use my recipes is that you mix it up a little. If the recipe calls for chops and you see a fresh ham steak, use that instead. If you find a shoulder—half or whole, bone-in or boned—consider cutting the primary muscles out with a fillet knife and slicing them into irregular steaks. Buy a whole shoulder and cut the meat into smaller steaks, using the leftover chunks for stewing—there are plenty of recipes here that call for cubed shoulder. The meat will be delicious, and so long as you work around the connective tissue between the muscles, you'll find the meat flavorful and rich. I promise you'll like the results; just don't expect the meat to have the exact same tame pliability as tenderloin.

NATURAL, ANTIBIOTIC-FREE, AND ORGANIC

Most people now understand just how meaning-less the term "natural" is when it comes to food labels, including meat of all kinds.

The "natural" label simply indicates that the meat contains a minimum of additives: no artificial colorings, flavorings, or preservatives. But, unless the label says "antibiotic-free" or "raised without the use of antibiotics," you can be pretty sure the "natural" pork you're looking at was regularly fed rather shocking quantities of antibiotics. These drugs both protect the health of the animal in profoundly unhealthful, overcrowded conditions and promote the pig's rapid growth. I strongly recommend you seek out better-quality pork.

Most larger supermarkets carry either organic pork or pork that, although not organic, has been raised without the use of antibiotics. Usually, these animals mature under conditions that are considerably healthier and cleaner than those of conventionally raised ani-mals. As much of an improvement as this pork is, you can do better by seeking out certified organic pork (labeled USDA Organic) or, even better, a local farmer who's serious about raising succulent, flavorful pork. The meat may not be cer-tified organic, but the animals will almost certainly be fed a diverse diet of grain, fruit, and scraps, while living a social existence with access to the outdoors and plenty of fresh air. This happy, active pig's life results in mark-edly superior meat.

FRESHNESS

Buy your pork with a "use by," "sell by," or "best if used by" date that falls in the future, not on the day of or on the day after you purchase it. (Each term means something slightly different but the point stands.) The reality is that meat is often subject to less than optimal conditions on the way to and at the grocery (above 40°F/4°C, which should be the maximum temperature). This gives the inevitable bacteria on the meat (really, all meat has bacteria, good and bad) the opportunity to reproduce. This is particularly true of vacuum-packed (no oxygen) pork or pork in modified atmosphere packaging (MAP). The use-by date on this airtight packaging is determined by the manufacturer—often falling as many as forty-five days after the meat was packed. The truth is, this is simply too optimistic, given the variable conditions in which the meat is kept, its pH level, and the initial bacterial load, however large or small it might be. The result may be slimy, slightly stinky meat. I doubt I need to emphasize that you should not eat any meat that smells even slightly "off." The odor your pork exudes should be virtually nonexistent—in other words, clean. The texture of the exterior should not be slippery or even vaguely slimy—if it is, what you're feeling is the evidence of bacteria at work. Meat under occupation by an army of microbes, inside and on the surface, doesn't belong in your kitchen, much less on your plate.

FROZEN PORK

Fresh pork, like fresh beef, fish, or chicken, is not the same as frozen. Unfortunately, if you buy most of your meat from a farmer, as I do, you'll almost certainly be buying frozen meat. Most farmers slaughter their animals once a month or even less frequently. That means if you want to buy meat more than once a month, you'll need to accept the frozen product. Given the scarcity of butchering facilities, most commercial butchering operations used by small farmers cut, seal, and flash-freeze the meat before delivering it back to the farmer.

I have a small freezer chest in my basement, which enables me to stock up on great

meat, albeit frozen. Much of the pork I cooked to write this book came from about 10 mi/16 km away, near the town of Pipersville, Pennsylvania. There, Joanna and Marc Michini run a small operation called Purley Farm. They are family farmers, if there ever were such a thing, and yet they're serious scientists when it comes to raising their animals. The animals are fed for optimal health, flavor, and marbling, and they're slaughtered with extreme care, according to customer specification—if the customer asks. I'm big on pork belly, so I ask for as much as I can get. They set a bunch aside for me, since most pork belly is cured and smoked for bacon. I also request heads and trotters whenever I want them.

If you don't have access to farmers, it's worth making the trip to the nearest source. Fill your freezer. Whole Foods and other natural foods markets sell fresh certified organic and hormone-free pork from a range of reliable sources. If you have one nearby, all I can do is envy you from afar.

THAWING

The best way to thaw pork is sealed (use a ziplock if your meat is not already vacuum packed) and then submerged in cold water, which conducts heat far better than air. A full-size pork butt can take days to thaw in the refrigerator, but if you can submerge it in water, you'll have it thawed out in less than half the time. As always, be very careful not to allow your meat to remain above 40°F/4°C for more than an hour or two. You can add ice cubes to the water bath, thaw the meat in a refrigerator, or both if you're working with a large piece of meat. (I use a cooler filled with ice-water brine.) Remember, the bacteria on the exterior of the meat will get busy reproducing as soon as the temperature is favorable, even if the center of the meat remains safely frozen.

For smaller cuts, like chops, ham steaks, and belly, a warm water bath works its magic in under an hour, enabling you to cook the meat right away without any worry or possibility of spoilage. Better yet, make that water bath a brining solution (see following), and you'll be making your pork more delicious while it thaws.

HOW TO COOK PORK

To my mind, there are only two ways to cook pork—long and slow or with a quick sear and a lower temperature to finish. Each has its place and purpose, depending on the cut and the cook's goal.

As Harold McGee, my favorite food science guru, writes in *On Food and Cooking*, "As the meat's temperature rises to 140°F/60°C, more of the proteins inside its cells coagulate and the cells become more segregated into a solid core of coagulated protein and a surrounding tube of liquid: so the meat gets progressively firmer and moister. Then between 140 and 150°F/60 and 65°C, the meat suddenly releases lots of juice, shrinks noticeably, and becomes chewier." As he notes, "if the cooking continues, the meat will get progressively drier, more compacted, and stiff."

Generally, tougher cuts like ribs, whole shoulders, and hams are slow cooked to break down the ample collagen, turning it to gelatin. (The fat in these cuts keeps the meat tasty, along with your mop or sauce.) Slow cooking optimally occurs when you cook your meat, whether it's in the oven, grill, or smoker, at 200 to 250°F/95 to 120°C. This gentle heat allows the meat to cook for a long time (up to twelve hours) without burning. When properly cooked, the internal temperature of a smoked pork shoulder for pulled pork should be between 180 and 190°F/80 and 88°C.

For tender cuts, faster high-temperature cooking is optimal because your goal is to keep the fibers tender while minimizing moisture loss. With pork, as with a steak, you want to brown the exterior as much as possible without completely cooking the meat, and then move to moderate heat to finish the cooking process. Juicy, succulent meat is perceived this way in part because it's fattier (fat coats meat fibers, lubricating the feel of them in the mouth) and in part because it does contain more of the liquid that makes up about 75 percent of meat.

Keep in mind that dry, mealy meat (unfortunately, so common) is the end result of lean pork that's been overcooked. The optimal internal temperature for any meat you're not slow cooking should be around 145°F/63°C. The most common mistake home cooks (and some professionals!) make when cooking pork (often from the loin section) is overcooking out of fear of pink meat, which we all grew up thinking was dangerous because of trichinosis. (The parasite poses a very minor risk today. See Food Safety and the Dangers of Undercooked Meat, facing page.)

BRINING

Whether you're panfrying, roasting, grilling, or slow cooking, the best way to insure your meat retains optimal moisture is by brining it in a 5 to 6 percent salt solution. The effect of saltwater is twofold. First (again, according to McGee), the meat gains about 10 percent of its weight in water as the cells plump, retaining more water thanks to the salt in the solution. Second, salt disrupts the structure of the muscle filaments and the proteins that hold those filaments together, making the meat more tender.

All in all, I'm a big proponent of brining pork (and chicken!). It's easy, and you don't necessarily need to plan ahead. Brine any and all recipes you find here; just beware of oversalting before tasting your meat. To brine, combine 1 tbsp salt per 1 cup/240 ml cold water and submerge the meat in the solution for 1 hour or so at room temperature prior to cooking, or for up to 24 hours refrigerated. Better yet, begin with a warm brining solution (about 100°F/38°C) and do not refrigerate. If you do this, just be sure to cook the meat within 1 hour from the time you remove it from the brine as, given enough time, bacteria will thrive at this temperature.

FOOD SAFETY AND THE DANGERS OF UNDERCOOKED MEAT

Many people cook their pork well beyond the slightest hint of pink to avoid trichinosis. You should know that between 2008 and 2010 only twenty cases of this parasitic disease were reported to the Centers for Disease Control and Prevention (CDC) in the United States. Most of these were the result of undercooked bear or other game meat—not pork. In addition, pork that has been frozen will not contain *Trichinella spiralis*, the most common form of trichinosis in pigs.

There are, of course, other dangers to eating raw or undercooked pork, but the surface of your meat, when cooked with virtually any method, will reach 160°F/71°C, the magic number for killing a range of food-borne bacteria lurking there. The following are the most common ones you need to combat:

Escherichia coli (E. coli), Staphylococcus aureus (staph), Yersinia enterocolitica, and *Listeria monocytogenes*. Proper handling of raw meat will inhibit the growth of these bacteria, and adequate cooking will kill them. Don't worry, even if you cook your meat low and slow at 200°F/95°C, you'll kill these nasty buggers. Ground pork is another matter and should be cooked through so that all parts reach the magic pathogen-killing 160°F/71°C.

REMOVING THE SILVERSKIN FROM A TENDERLOIN AND RIBS

Be sure to remove the pesky membrane, called the silverskin, that coats the tenderloin and covers the underside of ribs. It prevents the rub or marinade from penetrating the meat. Shiny, thin, and difficult to see, it's usually there, whether it's visible to you or not. Try to get under it with your fingers or a paring knife and then use your hands to pull at it. The fresher the ribs, the easier it will be to remove, often tearing off in one big, gratifying pull. If you're having difficulty or you're preparing slab upon slab of ribs at once and your fingers are getting numb, use a paper towel to grip the thin, slippery nuisance.

ROASTING

To roast a large cut of meat, you want to focus on browning the exterior while cooking the interior slowly to 145°F/63°C. I recommend browning a big roast for 20 minutes at 400°F/200°C and then turning the oven down to a relatively moderate 300°F/150°C to finish cooking the interior. If you have time, you'll get very nice results by turning the oven down as low as 200°F/95°C, but if a roast takes 30 to 40 minutes to finish cooking at 300°F/150°C, it will take nearly twice as long at 200°F/95°C. Always allow your meat to sit at room temperature for at least 30 minutes before cooking (or brine it in room-temperature water). When it's ready to go in the oven, dry your meat thoroughly and rub it all over with organic high-heat oil (see High-Temperature Cooking Oils, facing page) and salt.

OVEN SLOW COOKING

The magic of slow cooking in the oven can't be overstated. Try sticking a pork belly or some well-seasoned ribs in the oven for 3 to 4 hours at 200°F/95°C, and you'll see what I mean. Sure, you won't get the smoky flavor that comes from slow cooking on the grill, but in winter, when it's 20°F/-7°C out and you need some ribs (it happens), this method can save you. The greatest virtue of roasting at 200°F/95°C is that you have to really try to burn or dry out the meat at this temperature; the heat is so moderate that you can just turn on the oven, put the meat in, and walk away, without worrying about returning to a blackened disaster. I don't put water in the bottom of my roasting pan when using this method because I really hate the smell and taste of steamed pork.

BRAISING

Pork takes to braising better than most proteins. Because pork is almost always skinless, the loss of crispy skin is not a concern as it is with chicken; and unlike with beef, that lusty rare center is never desirable. When pork is braised, the fat and connective tissue melt slowly as the meat cooks gently in liquid, which never exceeds the ideal braising temperature of 212°F/100°C. Ask any pit master the optimal temperature for slow cooking, and he or she is sure to tell you this is the divine number. You can't go wrong.

GRILLING

A chop thrown on a hot grill to soak up a little smoke and take on a nice charred exterior is a happy indulgence. When it comes to pork, the trick to getting it right is avoiding too hot a fire, which is sure to overcook your delicate chop or ham steak. The other problem with grilling pork over direct heat is that fat will drip all over your coals, creating massive flare-ups. By cooking just off to the side of direct heat, you'll get color without extreme heat. If you aren't getting the color you want this way, or if you're using a gas grill with no space to cook indirectly, take your time and watch the meat carefully. In this case, the best option may be to allow your meat to finish cooking in a warming oven. You'll have juicy, tender meat rather than the mealy, dry texture that evokes the dreaded phrase "the other white meat."

PANFRYING

I like to panfry, even though my exhaust fan consists of a serious cross draft in my kitchen, thanks to windows on three sides. Cooking pork with a little fat in a heavy cast-iron pan gives you plenty of control over doneness and browning if you pay attention. I like this easy, fast method for almost any kind of chop and even for browning tenderloins before finishing them in a low oven (I do the same with thick chops).

CHOOSING OILS FOR COOKING

If there's a subject among home cooks and chefs that has limitless potential for debate, cooking oil is right up there—particularly high-heat oil. It's fairly easy to agree on the best oil for salads or even for low-temperature cooking, like sautéing vegetables or frying an egg. But when the time comes to crank the burner up to its highest setting and smoke up the kitchen as meat browns or a bunch of vegetables and pork belly crisp in the wok, things can get pretty contentious. Over the years, I've done as much research on oil as I could while at the same time testing my findings in my own kitchen. Here, I explain my choices and the logic behind them. I hope it helps you make solid decisions in your own kitchen that are driven by science. As I found, tradition and plain old bad habits can lead you astray.

HIGH-TEMPERATURE COOKING OILS

When I call for "organic high-heat oil" in my recipes, I mean any of the following: canola, peanut, safflower, sunflower, soy, avocado, rice bran, and almond oils. They're all available in cold-pressed, organic form, suitable for high-temperature cooking. (Surprisingly, grape seed oil has a lower smoke point than the oils listed above.)

In short, if you're looking for a healthful oil that balances smoke point, good fats, and the least toxic refinement process, look for an oil that says right on the label "expeller pressed," which is another way

of saying "mechanically pressed." You also want to look for the small, round, green-and-white USDA Organic seal, which ensures the refinement process doesn't involve scary bleaching and deodorizing processes. Finally, the oil you use should be labeled "Refined for High Heat" and show a temperature gauge on the back of the label with an arrow pointing to the red "High Heat" or "High Heat Up to 450°F/230°C."

The controversy over choosing the best high-heat oil is mostly about the source of the fat, what sorts of compounds and fatty acids it does or doesn't contain, and how it's been processed and refined. You want oil with plenty of omega-6 and omega-9 fatty acids. You don't want oil that has been derived or refined using obscure chemicals nor do you want those chemicals used in the deodorizing process. You also want to avoid artery-clogging partially or fully hydrogenated fats.

For browning meat, deep-frying, high-temperature roasting, and cooking in a wok, you need an oil with a high smoke point (425 to 450°F/220 to 230°C), not just because you don't want to set off the smoke alarm but also because when oil burns and smokes, it release unhealthful free radicals and fumes. Breathing these fumes and consuming the oil after it's been subjected to this sort of heat is less than ideal, particularly if the oil is chemically processed or poorly suited to high heat in the first place.

The oils most people use look okay at first glance, but unless they're mechanically pressed, they're a little scary because they've undergone harsh chemical refinement to make them pure enough to handle high heat. (A side of hexane solvent, anyone?) The most common oil, highly refined "vegetable" oil (usually derived from soy in North America), has a high smoke point and it's cheap. But it's not necessarily what you want to be putting in your body or breathing in smoke form every day, year after year. Ditto with palm oil and peanut oil, which have their own set of issues, including pesticide contamination.

The plant source an oil is extracted from and the extent to which it has been refined dictate its crucial flash or smoke point. The degree of refinement also determines flavor, to a certain extent. Highly refined olive oil, for example, is nearly flavorless, while less refined extra-virgin and unfiltered fruit or vegetable oils can be pungent and green, with a fruity, light acidity heightened by peppery notes. (Beware that many olive oils that claim to be extra-virgin are not.)

That's why I recommend you use highly refined, organic, cold-processed oil made from vegetables, legumes, or fruit, with a very high smoke point. Maybe one or two oils at your grocery store will meet the criteria, but plenty at the health food store or at a Whole Foods will.

In my kitchen these days, the more I learn the less I use my old standby, peanut oil. Instead, I use canola (rapeseed) oil (third-party-certified GMO-free, too, if you care). I also use highly refined organic avocado oil (harder to find and more expensive). Whatever you buy, it should meet the preceding criteria for processing, organic certification, and healthy fats.

Other options include virgin coconut oil (useful for many Asian dishes), but it does not have all that high a smoke point. Although lard does not have a super-high smoke point either, it is tasty and free. (I get it in the form of pig fat rendered from organic fatback or meat. When I cook pork belly in the oven, I save the rendered fat,

storing it in a little tub in the refrigerator. Ditto for bacon, but it has a distinctively smoky flavor, which may or may not be desirable, depending on your recipe.)

OLIVE OIL

As for olive oil, you should have one bottle for salads and for finishing meats or vegetables and another, more refined oil for lower-temperature cooking. I call for both in my recipes by listing "best olive oil" and "refined olive oil." Fruity, acidic, and complex in flavor, your "best" finishing oil will be first expeller cold pressed, and it will usually have a date and source on the bottle. My best olive oil usually comes from California or Italy. Your second-class, everyday "refined olive oil" will be somewhat flavorless and much lighter in color, but it will have a much higher smoke point (around 325°F/165°C). This relatively inexpensive oil is useful and healthful for a quick sauté of vegetables, but it's not good for high-temperature roasting or for browning meat. Again, look for certified organic, not so much for the sake of how the olives were grown (as nice as it is to know the olives are grown organically), but for the sake of the refinement process.

ON TOASTING SEEDS, NUTS, AND SPICES

Toasting seeds, nuts, and spices releases their oils, making them fragrant and flavorful. I like to heat a dry cast-iron pan over medium heat and, when it's hot, add my nuts, spices, or seeds. I then stand there shaking the pan and observing their progress from raw to cooked using my key senses—sight and smell. Look for a light browning and the fragrant smell that virtually all nuts and seeds exude when heated. For large batches of nuts or for coconut, use the oven, set on a moderate 300°F/150°C. Spread out the ingredient you're working with on a baking sheet and set a timer for 3 minutes. After that, check frequently; the window between raw and burned is painfully brief.

TOOLS AND EQUIPMENT YOU NEED

If you're cooking a lot of pork, a charcoal- or wood-burning grill with a cover or a full-on smoker is a beautiful thing to own. Plenty of hardwood charcoal, combined with wood chips, will produce a flavor-enhancing smoke that can't be duplicated. Can you make great ribs and even pulled pork in the oven? Sure. Will a gas grill do in a pinch? Definitely. But your meat will be missing the dynamic flavor of that magic smoke.

For cooking indoors, I couldn't live without a whole set of cast-iron pans. I own five, including a skillet. The largest is 12 in/ 30.5 cm and the smallest about 6 in/15 cm. They're inexpensive, retain heat, and disperse it better than any other material. Get one now. Finally, my life would be more complicated without a digital, instant-read thermometer, which, unlike the kind with a dial, gives a more accurate temperature and fast. Get one—they're not expensive.

For sauces, it helps to own a decent blender. A food processor with a standard blade, slicer, and small shredding attachment makes all that blending of sauces and pastes, slicing of vegetables for salads, and shredding of carrots and cabbage for slaw effortless. If you're old-school, a mortar and pestle is an excellent tool for gently crushing spices and muddling curry bases, but a spice grinder is fast and easy.

These recipes have been tested on a powerful (but not commercial) gas range. If your stove is a little old or lame (I've been there), you may need to increase the cooking time. Ditto for your oven. Finally, I'll add that if you cook more than once a week, it's worth owning at least one high-quality knife and keeping it sharp, however you can manage it. (High-quality knives stay sharp longer.) Get some advice at a good kitchen store, hold your breath, and hand over the cash. You won't regret it.

CHAPTER 1

AMERICAN PORK

AMERICAN PORK

All the recipes in this book are, of course, American in some sense. What distinguishes the ones in this chapter is that they are more fully assimilated into that rich stew that defines what I think of as American cuisine. Rather than holding to their origins in any discernible way, as do the recipes in the other chapters, the foods here are modern derivations of dishes, ingredients, and flavors rooted in Southern traditions, California cuisine, and Anglo-European cooking. I make no apologies for the seeming cultural imperialism of calling the food in this chapter American, with its implication that the food in the other chapters is somehow less American. Far from it. Quite simply, American is simply one more regional abstraction from which to cull dominant flavors and ingredients.

DRINKS

I like to drink wine with half the food in this chapter and beer with the other half. In general, I prefer to drink beer when I'm eating anything that might reasonably be called barbecue—it just seems right. For the remainder, wine would be my choice, as the recipes are generally not spicy and will be complemented by a range of wines (and vice versa), depending on the preparation.

Red or white wine with pork? It depends as much on the season as on the recipe. I wouldn't drink a heavy red like a Cabernet with any of the recipes here—with the notable exception of meat loaf. For the recipes that call for apples or pears, I'd push you toward a dry Riesling, which will bring out the fruit notes beautifully. For bigger, more dominant flavors like barbecued ribs or pulled pork, if you don't like beer, I'd suggest a Sauvignon Blanc or a blend with good acidity and some fruit. I like many Sauvignon Blancs and Rieslings from New Zealand. An inexpensive French bottle, blended or straight up, would also do nicely—maybe a young Sancerre or a blended white Rhône.

ON THE TABLE

I'm a bread hog. If I can find a well-crafted, sour, chewy baguette or *pain de seigle*, I never turn it down. Sweet butter served cold with a good loaf is never unwelcome if you're eating a chop or a roast with sides. Don't neglect the salt; flaky salt such as Maldon in a pretty little bowl is ideal, but I also like the standard kosher salt I cook with and some sea salts, so long as the grain is not too hard or large. For Southern food you don't want to neglect the bottle of hot sauce—as many as possible, since there is a great variety of them and everyone has a favorite. For the food in this chapter and the next, mine is Marie Sharp's from Belize.

SWEETS

Southern food is an invitation to make a classic fruit pie. Don't cheat by using a store-bought crust or filling, and you'll have the tastiest dessert, even if it doesn't look perfect. If you're not up to a pie, banana pudding is easy and crazy delicious; you know, layers of Nilla Wafers, vanilla custard (make your own!), sliced bananas, and whipped cream, all set in a glass like trifle—hard to resist even after eating too many ribs. For something more sophisticated, make a batch of shortbread cookies with a few herbs (thyme is my favorite), and sprinkle them with sea salt. This is by far my favorite dessert when served with super-high-quality dark chocolate. (Although I hate to admit it, I also love milk chocolate; the best is from Sweden and Norway.)

SHOULDER ROAST
WITH CRANBERRY KETCHUP, WILD RICE WITH CARAMELIZED ONIONS, AND BABY KALE SALAD

SERVES 4

I like the natural affinity of cranberries and wild rice. It's the union born of two plants that might easily have grown side by side in a wild bog. Bring on the rich, succulent pork, and you have an earthy meal worthy of Thanksgiving. (Although even my pork-lusting soul knows it would be heresy to skip the turkey on T-Day.)

— SHOULDER ROAST —

ONE 3- TO 4-LB/1.4- TO 1.8-KG BONE-IN SHOULDER ROAST

1 TBSP ORGANIC HIGH-HEAT OIL (SEE HIGH-TEMPERATURE COOKING OILS, PAGE 17)

1 TO 2 TSP KOSHER SALT

BLACK PEPPER

FLAKY SALT FOR FINISHING

Preheat the oven to 400°F/200°C. Take the roast out of the refrigerator 1 hour before you plan to begin roasting it. Dry it and rub it all over with the oil, kosher salt, and black pepper. Place it in a large cast-iron pan or a small roasting pan, roast for 15 minutes, and turn the oven down to 300°F/150°C. Cook for another 30 minutes before testing the temperature of the meat at its center. You want the meat around 140°F/60°C when you take it out of the oven. (It will gain several degrees as it rests on the counter.)

Carve the meat after letting it sit for 5 minutes, sprinkle with a little flaky salt and black pepper, and serve.

— CRANBERRY KETCHUP —

I have a love-hate relationship with Thanksgiving cranberry sauce. I'm attached to the recipe my mom, Pat, passed along, which essentially involves dumping a bag of raw cranberries in a pot, along with a whole tangerine or two, and covering it with orange juice. The powerfully acidic mixture is then cooked long enough to ruin the pot before you add a tad of sugar. Here, I've taken the spirit of that dish, added some garlic and shallot, and tried to ensure that you won't ruin a good pot by cutting down on the cooking time (use uncoated stainless steel to be safe). This sauce, which I like to call ketchup to put some distance between it and Thanksgiving, is a balance of tart berries, pungent garlic, and spice.

1½ CUPS/180 G FRESH CRANBERRIES (FROZEN WILL DO IN A PINCH)

3 CUPS/720 ML FRESH ORANGE JUICE

1 CINNAMON STICK

½ TSP GROUND CLOVES

¾ CUP/150 G SUGAR

2 TBSP BUTTER

1 LARGE SHALLOT, MINCED

½ TSP KOSHER SALT

3 GARLIC CLOVES

In a medium stainless-steel saucepan set over low heat, combine the cranberries, orange juice, cinnamon stick, cloves, and sugar. Bring the mixture to a simmer and cook, uncovered, for 2 hours, or until you have a thick, jammy consistency. Stir frequently at this stage or you will have a scorched pot (you may have one, anyway).

Meanwhile, combine the butter, shallot, and salt in a small frying pan set over low heat and cook, stirring frequently, for 8 to 10 minutes, or until the shallot is soft. Add the garlic and cook for another 3 to 5 minutes without browning it. Remove from the heat and add to the cranberry mixture. Stir and taste. I prefer this sauce warm and fragrant, but it's almost as good at room temperature. Leftover sauce will keep, refrigerated, for 10 days or so.

— WILD RICE WITH CARAMELIZED ONIONS —

I have a weakness for this weedy, grassy, and earthy "rice." (As you probably know, genus-wise, wild rice is a kissing cousin to rice—close, but not too close.) Revel in its chewy texture and the look of distinct long grains on your plate. Be sure to run some rice around in the cranberry ketchup—they're made for each other.

1 CUP/170 G WILD RICE

4 CUPS/960 ML WATER

1/2 TSP KOSHER SALT

3 TBSP BUTTER

1 LARGE SWEET YELLOW ONION, SUCH AS VIDALIA, COARSELY CHOPPED

1 TBSP CELERY SEED

FLAKY SALT AND BLACK PEPPER FOR FINISHING

In a medium saucepan with a lid set over medium heat, combine the rice, water, and kosher salt. Bring to a rapid boil, turn the heat to low, cover tightly, and cook for 45 to 55 minutes, or until the rice is tender and the water has been absorbed. While the rice is cooking, melt 2 tbsp of the butter in a medium sauté pan set over medium-low heat, add the onion and celery seed, and cook, stirring frequently, for 10 to 12 minutes, or until the onion is soft and translucent. Stir the onion mixture into the rice, and toss with the remaining tbsp butter, a pinch of flaky salt, and a grind of pepper. Serve hot.

— BABY KALE SALAD —

More and more widely available commercially, baby kale is an agreeable change from other lettuces, no matter how beloved. Add a little cheese—crumbled, grated, shaved, or cubed. I'm thinking goat, sheep, cow, or a mix of all three!

5 OZ/140 G BABY KALE

1/2 CUP/55 G CHOPPED WALNUTS, TOASTED

1/2 TSP KOSHER SALT

2 TBSP BEST OLIVE OIL (SEE OLIVE OIL, PAGE 18)

1 TBSP CIDER VINEGAR

BLACK PEPPER

In a large mixing or serving bowl, thoroughly toss together the kale, walnuts, salt, olive oil, and vinegar. Add a generous grind of black pepper and serve.

SHOULDER ROAST WITH ROSEMARY AND GARLIC,
COLLARD RIBBONS, AND CRISPY LEMON-SCENTED EGGPLANT

SERVES 4 TO 6

Whatever sort of roast you have, this method will work. By browning the exterior of the meat in a hot oven and then lowering the heat to gently finish the cooking process, the center of the roast comes out moist and tender. Be sure to test the roast after an hour if you have a smaller piece of meat, or if you have a cut from the loin, such as a rib roast, since leaner meat is less forgiving of over-cooking. This potent rub, which doubles as a sauce, is flavorful and bright, as is the Crispy Lemon-Scented Eggplant—a discovery for a non-eggplant-lover like me. The Collard Ribbons make the whole into a deeply satisfying meal.

— SHOULDER ROAST WITH ROSEMARY — AND GARLIC

ONE 4- TO 5-LB/1.8- TO 2.3-KG SHOULDER ROAST

2 GARLIC CLOVES, MINCED

2 SPRIGS FRESH ROSEMARY, FINELY CHOPPED

GRATED ZEST OF 1 LEMON

2 TBSP CAPERS, FINELY CHOPPED

1 LARGE SHALLOT, FINELY CHOPPED

4 ANCHOVY FILLETS, FINELY CHOPPED

1 TSP KOSHER SALT

2 TBSP ORGANIC REFINED OLIVE OIL (SEE OLIVE OIL, PAGE 18)

1/2 TSP CAYENNE PEPPER

Preheat the oven to 400°F/200°C. Dry the meat and rest it for 30 minutes to 1 hour at room temperature to take the chill off. Combine the garlic, rosemary, lemon zest, capers, shallot, anchovy, salt, olive oil, and cayenne in a small bowl and mash the ingredients together with a fork. Leave half the mixture in the bowl and set it aside. Use the rest to rub the meat all over, working it into the nooks and crannies and between the muscles. (There should be plenty of room between the muscle groups if you have a boneless roast.) Tie a couple of rounds of butcher's string around the meat so that it holds its shape, and set in a large cast-iron frying pan, a Dutch oven, or a small roasting pan.

Roast for 20 minutes and turn the oven down to 300°F/150°C. Cook the meat for 30 minutes more before checking the internal temperature (it won't be done unless you have a much smaller roast). You want the meat around 145°F/63°C. Cook for another 10 to 15 minutes and check again. (A very large roast may take up to 2 hours.) Allow the meat to rest for 5 minutes before carving. Smear the remaining herb mixture on the meat and serve.

— COLLARD RIBBONS —

This method made me a convert to one of the few leafy greens I didn't used to like much. Forget the dun-colored mass of overcooked leaves—these greens are fresh and tasty and may just change your mind about how to eat collards.

1 LARGE BUNCH COLLARDS, WASHED BUT NOT DRIED

3 TBSP OLIVE OIL

1 TBSP WATER

1 TSP KOSHER SALT

3 GARLIC CLOVES, SLICED

Rib the collard leaves with a sharp knife and discard the center and bottom stem. Working in batches, roll a large stack of greens into a tube and cut crosswise to make thin ribbons.

In a large saucepan over medium-high heat, combine the olive oil, water, collards, salt, and garlic. When you can hear the oil begin to sizzle, begin turning the greens over with tongs. They'll quickly lose volume, at which point you can stir them more easily. Cook for a total of 3 to 4 minutes—they should be bright green but wilted and fragrant with garlic. Serve immediately.

— CRISPY LEMON-SCENTED EGGPLANT —

I'm not the biggest fan of eggplant. Too often it's either
undercooked or undersalted, leaving that acrid taste on
your tongue that won't go away. This is the antidote to that
problem, and even better, it's crispy, bright, and surprisingly
irresistible. Achieving that crispy texture does, however,
require an overnight soak, so plan ahead.

2 LARGE PURPLE ITALIAN EGGPLANTS, WITH
THE CENTRAL CORE OF SEEDS CUT AWAY
(THE REMAINING SEEDS ARE FINE)

2 TBSP KOSHER SALT

1/4 CUP/60 ML ORGANIC REFINED OLIVE OIL
(SEE OLIVE OIL, PAGE 18)

1/2 LEMON

1/4 CUP/10 G CHOPPED FRESH PARSLEY

FLAKY OR COARSE SALT (OPTIONAL)

Using the slicer attachment for your food processor, cut the eggplants into thin ribbons. In a mixing bowl or a storage container
with a lid, combine the salt and eggplant. Mix and refrigerate for
24 to 48 hours.

Remove the eggplants from the refrigerator and drain off any visible liquid. Using an immaculate dish towel (or your bare hands),
squeeze the eggplants to remove as much liquid as you can.

Heat the olive oil in a large frying pan over medium heat. Sauté
the eggplants for 20 to 25 minutes, stirring occasionally. The eggplants are done when browned and crisped around the edges—they
should look almost like sautéed mushrooms. Transfer the eggplants
to a serving bowl and juice the lemon half over them. Sprinkle
with the parsley and, if needed, add a pinch or two of flaky salt
before serving.

SAUTÉED CHOPS WITH CIDER REDUCTION, CABBAGE AND APPLES, AND THYME-SCENTED POTATO GRATIN

SERVES 4

For ages—until the advent of modern refrigeration in the last century—pigs were slaughtered in autumn. Fattened on grain, acorns, and whatever else was up for grabs amid the harvest abundance, any pork that wasn't salted, smoked, and cured was eaten fresh. Since apple season also arrives in fall, the pairing of pork and apples feels intuitive—and it is. Our ancestors have been eating the two together for so long, it's coded into our genes. Here, the sweet apple is tempered by the sour cabbage. The meal as a whole is elevated by the richest, most decadent gratin I know.

— SAUTÉED CHOPS WITH CIDER REDUCTION —

FOUR 12- TO 16-OZ/340- TO 455-G BONE-IN, CENTER-CUT CHOPS

ORGANIC HIGH-HEAT OIL FOR COATING THE CHOPS, PLUS 1 TBSP (SEE HIGH-TEMPERATURE COOKING OILS, PAGE 17)

1 TSP KOSHER SALT

2 TBSP BUTTER

1 CUP/240 ML FRESHLY PRESSED APPLE CIDER (NOT JUICE)

FLAKY SALT AND BLACK PEPPER FOR FINISHING

Preheat the oven to 300°F/150°C. Dry the chops all over, coat with a little oil and the kosher salt, and set to rest on the counter for 30 minutes to 1 hour to take the chill off.

Heat a large cast-iron pan over high heat, add the 1 tbsp oil and, when it shimmers, carefully place the chops in the pan. Cook for 3 to 5 minutes on the first side and 2 to 3 minutes on the second to brown the exterior. Place in the oven, pan and all, for 5 to 10 minutes, or until the internal temperature reaches 145°F/63°C. (Thick-cut 1½-in/4-cm chops may take another 5 minutes or so.) The meat is done when it's pink but not bloody and the texture is lightly granular, not slippery and smooth as it is when it's raw.

Place the chops on a platter (don't wash that pan), turn the oven off, crack the oven door, and place the chops inside to rest while you make your sauce. Add the butter and cider to the pan over medium-high heat, scraping up the brown bits on the bottom with a spatula. Lower the heat to medium and reduce the cider for 5 to 8 minutes, or until it's the color of caramel on an apple and the spatula leaves a space behind it when you push it through the sauce. The sauce should be the consistency of warm honey. Pour the sauce over the chops, finish with a pinch of flaky salt and a little black pepper, and serve.

— CABBAGE AND APPLES —

A classic combination—this version is buttery, with a hint of onion and mustard. It is pork's best ally.

2 TBSP BUTTER

1 SWEET YELLOW ONION, SUCH AS VIDALIA, THINLY SLICED

1 TBSP GRAINY MUSTARD

½ CUP/120 ML CIDER VINEGAR (BRAGG'S HAS GREAT FLAVOR)

½ LARGE HEAD GREEN CABBAGE, THINLY SLICED (NOT SHREDDED)

1 SOUR APPLE, PEEL ON, CORED AND THINLY SLICED (I LIKE GINGER GOLD IN SEASON AND GRANNY SMITH THE REMAINDER OF THE YEAR)

½ TSP KOSHER SALT

In a large frying pan set over low heat, combine the butter and onion. Cook for 20 to 30 minutes, stirring frequently, until the onion has turned a deep caramel color and the slices stick together in the pan. Add the mustard, vinegar, cabbage, apple, and salt. Raise the heat to medium and cook for 20 to 25 minutes, stirring frequently. The cabbage and apples should be soft and browned in spots. Serve immediately.

— THYME-SCENTED POTATO GRATIN —

For a woodsy note amid the sweet and sour of the apples and
cabbage, I've added thyme to a raclette-potato-cream combination.
It's difficult to go terribly wrong here.

2 TSP BUTTER, AT ROOM TEMPERATURE

2 TBSP FRESH THYME LEAVES

8 TO 10 MEDIUM YUKON GOLD POTATOES,
PEELED AND SLICED VERY THIN

KOSHER SALT AND BLACK PEPPER

1 LB/455 G RACLETTE CHEESE, GRATED (SUBSTITUTE
COMTÉ OR GRUYÈRE FOR MORE BITE)

1½ CUPS/360 ML HEAVY CREAM

Preheat the oven to 400°F/200°C. Grease two 12-by-8-in/30.5-by-20-cm
oval casserole dishes or the equivalent with the butter. Sprinkle
the bottom of each dish with 1½ tsp of the thyme, and then lay the
potato slices down so that they just overlap. Sprinkle each with
a pinch of salt, a grind of pepper, another 1½ tsp thyme, and
about a sixth of the cheese. Repeat for another layer. For the
final layer, use all the remaining cheese and no thyme. Pour the
cream evenly over the top, dividing it between the two dishes.
Bake on the lower rack in the oven for 40 to 50 minutes, or until
the top is nicely browned all over and the bubbling cream is
visible only on the edges. (Don't worry if they won't both fit
on the bottom; just keep an eye on the browning of the one on the
upper rack and rotate if necessary.) If the gratins appear oily
when you take them from the oven, don't worry, they'll be fine;
the oil will reintegrate into the potatoes. Let them rest for
5 minutes or so to set before serving. I like to pass at the table
with a big spoon, letting everyone take as much as they like.

CHOPS
WITH OLIVE-FETA RELISH AND MARRAKESH COUSCOUS

SERVES 4

Any chop is best with a crusty brown exterior and a light pink interior. Getting there can be tricky, since pork is prone to drying out when overcooked. The idea here is to get the chop browned quickly, without cooking it through, and moving it to a warm oven to finish it.

— CHOPS —

FOUR 12-OZ TO 1-LB/340- TO 455-G BONE-IN, CENTER-CUT CHOPS

ORGANIC HIGH-HEAT OIL FOR COATING THE CHOPS, PLUS 1 TBSP (SEE HIGH-TEMPERATURE COOKING OILS, PAGE 17)

1 TSP KOSHER SALT

FLAKY SALT AND BLACK PEPPER FOR FINISHING

Preheat the oven to 300°F/150°C. (To grill, see the instructions on page 126.) Dry the chops all over, coat with a little oil and the kosher salt, and set on the counter for 1 hour to take the chill off.

Heat a large cast-iron pan over high heat, add the 1 tbsp oil and, when it shimmers, carefully place the chops in the pan. Cook for 3 to 5 minutes on the first side and 2 to 3 minutes on the second to brown the exterior. Set in the oven, pan and all, for 5 to 10 minutes, or until the internal temperature reaches 145°F/63°C. (Thick-cut 1½-in/4-cm chops may take another 5 minutes or so.) The meat is done when it's pink, but not bloody, and the texture is slightly granular, not slippery and smooth as it is when raw.

Finish with a pinch of flaky salt and a little black pepper and serve.

— OLIVE-FETA RELISH —

Pungent and reminiscent of the easy languor of a Mediterranean summer, this combination will brighten every flavor on your plate. Buy olives with pits—they're generally better quality, since the process of commercial pitting damages the fruit.

½ CUP/75 G KALAMATA OLIVES, PITTED AND COARSELY CHOPPED

3½ OZ/100 G SHEEP'S MILK FETA, CRUMBLED (VALBRESO IS MY FAVORITE)

½ CUP/20 G CHOPPED FRESH PARSLEY

2 TBSP CHOPPED FRESH OREGANO

1 TBSP CHOPPED FRESH ROSEMARY

2 TBSP BEST OLIVE OIL (SEE OLIVE OIL, PAGE 18)

2 TBSP FRESH LEMON JUICE

1 TSP RED PEPPER FLAKES

1 CUP/215 G CANNED CHICKPEAS, RINSED, DRAINED, AND CRUSHED

Combine all the ingredients in a small bowl. Stir well, cover, and allow to sit at room temperature for up to 1 hour to allow the flavors to blend and mellow before serving. If you make extra, store it, tightly sealed, in the refrigerator for up to 3 days.

— MARRAKESH COUSCOUS —

Buttery and decadent, this is a forcefully seductive side dish. Serve it at room temperature with an iced dry Riesling. The taste of the fruit and nuts will take on an unexpected complexity.

2 CUPS/480 ML WATER

2 CUPS/340 G MEDIUM-GRAIN COUSCOUS (ANY TYPE WILL DO; SIMPLY ADJUST THE COOKING TIME AND WATER ACCORDING TO PACKAGE INSTRUCTIONS)

10 DRIED APRICOTS, DRIED TART CHERRIES, OR A MIX, CHOPPED

¼ CUP/30 G SLICED ALMONDS

¼ CUP/30 G PISTACHIOS, SHELLED AND CHOPPED

2 TBSP FRESH LEMON JUICE

2 TBSP BUTTER, MELTED

2 TBSP BEST OLIVE OIL (SEE OLIVE OIL, PAGE 18)

¼ CUP/10 G CHOPPED FRESH MINT

¼ CUP/10 G CHOPPED FRESH OREGANO

1½ TSP KOSHER SALT

Bring the water to a boil in a saucepan with a lid over high heat. Add the couscous and remove from the heat. Cover and let it sit for 5 minutes, and then fluff with a fork. Stir in the apricots, almonds, pistachios, lemon juice, butter, olive oil, mint, oregano, and salt. Serve warm or at room temperature.

TENDERLOIN WITH SALSA VERDE,

CELERIAC-POTATO MASH, AND FENNEL-PARSLEY SALAD

SERVES 4

Slow cooking a tenderloin on the stove top and then dousing it with ample garlic and herbs suspended in this very flavorful green sauce transforms a simple loin into a spectacle. The salsa verde does triple duty as a marinade, a stuffing, and a sauce—an arrangement that is efficient and rewarding. The outrageously rich mash and Fennel-Parsley Salad make a brilliant match.

— TENDERLOIN WITH SALSA VERDE —

1 CUP/40 G MIXED FRESH MINT, BASIL, AND THYME LEAVES

½ CUP/120 ML ORGANIC REFINED OLIVE OIL (SEE OLIVE OIL, PAGE 18)

1 CHILE, DRIED OR FRESH

¼ CUP/60 ML FRESH LEMON JUICE

1 TSP KOSHER SALT

½ HEAD GARLIC

ONE 1-LB/455-G TENDERLOIN

1 TBSP ORGANIC HIGH-HEAT OIL (SEE HIGH-TEMPERATURE COOKING OILS, PAGE 17)

FLAKY SALT AND BLACK PEPPER FOR FINISHING

Combine the herbs, olive oil, chile, lemon juice, kosher salt, and garlic in a blender or food processor. Work until smooth. Dry the tenderloin and lay it on a cutting surface. Slit it lengthwise down the middle, cutting as deeply as possible without cutting it in half. Place the tenderloin, with its slit open, on a plate. Pour ¼ cup/60 ml green sauce into the center of the meat. Close up the meat to re-form into its original shape. Cut about 5 ft/1.5 m of butcher's string, encircle one end of the meat, and secure with a knot, leaving one long end trailing. Wrap the long end of string around the meat three or four times as you move down the tenderloin. Double back, crossing over the first round of string. Secure to the short end of the string from the original knot, and cut off any remaining string. Return the meat to the plate. Reserve $1/3$ cup/75 ml sauce, and drizzle on the remainder as a marinade. Let the meat stand on the counter for up to 1 hour, or cover and refrigerate for up to 24 hours. If you do refrigerate, let the meat stand at room temperature before cooking to take the chill off for 30 minutes to 1 hour.

Preheat the oven to 300°F/150°C. Heat a large cast-iron pan over high heat, add the high-heat oil and, when it shimmers, carefully place the loin in the pan. Cook for 3 to 5 minutes on the first side, rotate, and cook another 2 to 3 minutes to brown the exterior as evenly as possible. Set the meat in the oven, pan and all, for 12 to 15 minutes, or until the internal temperature reaches 145°F/63°C when an instant-read thermometer is inserted in the center. The loin is done when the meat is pink, but not bloody, and the texture slightly granular, not slippery and smooth as it is when raw. Remove the meat from the oven and let it rest for 5 minutes before slicing. To serve, cut away the string, slice the meat into rounds, and drizzle each portion with the reserved salsa verde, finishing with a pinch of flaky salt and some black pepper before serving.

— CELERIAC-POTATO MASH —

Celery root doesn't seduce or invite the cook. Don't be fooled. If you're apt to be put off by the knobby, dirty, gnarly root—don't. Once peeled and cooked until soft, this off-putting beast will reveal a creamy, flavorful center with the subtle yet distinctive taste of celery. You'll want a knife, not a peeler, to get these roots clean and ready to cook.

2 SMALL TO MEDIUM CELERY ROOTS, OR 1 LARGE ROOT, PEELED, RINSED, AND HALVED

6 MEDIUM YUKON GOLD POTATOES

$1^{1}/_{2}$ CUPS/360 ML HEAVY CREAM

3 TBSP BUTTER

1 TSP KOSHER SALT

BLACK PEPPER

Set a steamer basket in the bottom of a large saucepan with a tight-fitting lid and fill with water up to the base of the basket. Put the celery root in the basket, cover, and set over medium heat.

Cook for 20 minutes, and insert a paring knife into each root to test for doneness. The knife should slide right in, without resistance. Cook for an additional 5 or 10 minutes, if needed. Meanwhile, peel the potatoes, placing them, as you work, in a separate pot half filled with cold water. Cook over high heat for 20 to 25 minutes, or until a knife inserted into the center of the largest potato meets no resistance.

When the celery root and potatoes are cooked, drain and press them through a ricer or large food mill straight into the pot you cooked the potatoes in. Celery root is fibrous and will require some elbow grease. Discard the bits that won't go through the mill. Do not stir the potatoes or celery root. Heat the cream, butter, salt, and a generous grind of black pepper in a small saucepan over medium-low heat until the butter is melted and a skin forms on the cream. Watch that it doesn't boil over! Pour the hot cream mixture over the riced roots. Stir briefly, just enough to incorporate the cream, and taste for salt. Transfer to a warm serving bowl and serve.

— FENNEL-PARSLEY SALAD —

Parsley has come a long way since its main job was to sit preposterously in sad, curly sprigs on the edge of every hot plate in America. Today, parsley has quit that job in all but the most resolutely retro restaurants. (Salad bar, anyone?) Instead, it's found its destiny as a flavorful green in its own right. To experience this underappreciated herb at its best, eat a lot of it. You'll see what I mean.

1 LARGE BUNCH FRESH PARSLEY

1 FENNEL BULB, TRIMMED AND VERY THINLY SLICED (USE A MANDOLINE IF YOU HAVE ONE)

GRATED ZEST OF 1 LEMON, PREFERABLY ORGANIC

1 TO 2 TBSP FRESH LEMON JUICE

2 TBSP BEST OLIVE OIL (SEE OLIVE OIL, PAGE 18)

FLAKY SALT AND BLACK PEPPER

Float the parsley in a large mixing bowl filled with cold water to remove any grit. (Even the slightest crunch of sand spoils the salad.) Dry the parsley thoroughly and meticulously pick the leaves off the stems. In a salad bowl or mixing bowl, combine the parsley leaves and fennel. Add the lemon zest, lemon juice, olive oil, a pinch of salt, and a grind of black pepper. Toss and taste, adding salt (or lemon juice) as you see fit before serving.

SALT-AND-PEPPER
BABY BACKS
WITH BAKED CHEESE GRITS
AND CIDER VINEGAR SLAW

SERVES 4

I'm no Southerner, but in summer this is one of my favorite
meals. It never fails to bring me back to the Southern road trip
I took with my husband, Dwight, six months after we met. Other
than getting engaged—which we did over ribs, grits, beans, slaw,
and collards—we had no purpose other than faithfully seeking
out barbecue. Back then we used Jane and Michael Stern's *Roadfood*,
marking destinations in red ink right on our Rand McNally atlas.
We then drove in erratic zigzags from one smoky, backwoods joint
to another, following nothing more than the red dots on the
map to the promise of a seemingly endless future of food bliss.
You will need 2 or 3 handfuls hardwood chips, soaked in water
for 30 minutes or more and drained, for smoking the ribs.

— SALT-AND-PEPPER BABY BACKS —

4 TO 5 LB/1.8 TO 2.3 KG BABY BACK RIBS
(2 OR 3 SLABS), SILVERSKIN REMOVED
(SEE THE INSTRUCTIONS ON PAGE 15)

KOSHER SALT AND BLACK PEPPER

1 TO 2 TBSP ORGANIC HIGH-HEAT OIL (SEE HIGH-
TEMPERATURE COOKING OILS, PAGE 17)

YOUR FAVORITE HOT SAUCE FOR SERVING

Dry the ribs and rub all over with salt and plenty of black pepper.
Rub on a light gloss of oil.

Build a medium fire in a charcoal or wood grill or heat a gas grill to medium. If you're using charcoal or wood, you want hot embers, not flames. (If you don't have a grill large enough to place the meat away from the heat source, make a small fire or set the gas grill to its lowest setting.) Use a clean, well-cured grate. Place a handful of wood chips on the fire. Repeat every hour, adding charcoal or wood and wood chips to maintain the smoke and a steady temperature. Add fuel more frequently if the temperature of the grill dips below 200°F/95°C. It should hover between 200 and 350°F/95 and 180°C.

Lay the ribs on the grill over indirect heat, cover the grill, and cook for 2 to 3 hours, turning the ribs every 30 minutes or so. (If you prefer to roast the ribs in the oven, see the recipe on page 120 for instructions.) The ribs are done when they're brown and crispy and you can easily pull a bone from the rack. You can dry out ribs by overcooking them, so keep an eye on them and test frequently; all grills are different. Serve the ribs piled on a platter. Don't neglect to bring out the hot sauce.

— BAKED CHEESE GRITS —

I never use American cheese—sweet and uncheeselike as it is—except on my egg sandwiches. (I worship at the egg sandwich shrine.) Here, I've made an exception to my bendable rule by adding one slice of American cheese to these grits. It delivers a little sweetness while contributing to the creamy texture. This is a wildly tasty side and beautifully sidles right up next to the ribs and slaw, needing no more encouragement than a drop of hot sauce.

4 TBSP/55 G COLD BUTTER

1 LARGE SHALLOT, MINCED

2 GARLIC CLOVES, MINCED

1 CUP/135 G WHITE OR YELLOW STONE-GROUND GRITS (I LIKE ANSON MILLS BEST)

2 CUPS/480 ML WATER

2 CUPS/480 ML WHOLE MILK

1 1/2 TSP KOSHER SALT

1 TSP WORCESTERSHIRE SAUCE

1 1/4 CUPS/125 G GRATED SHARP CHEDDAR CHEESE

1 SLICE AMERICAN CHEESE

Preheat the oven to 400°F/200°C. Combine the butter, shallot, and garlic in a medium pot set over medium heat. Cook, stirring frequently, until the butter melts. Add the grits and stir to coat with the butter before adding the water, milk, salt, and Worcestershire. Mix thoroughly and cook over low heat for 20 to 25 minutes, stirring frequently with a spatula to scrape the bottom of the pot. The grits should be thick, but just liquid enough to pour. Add half the cheddar cheese and the American cheese, and stir until the cheese melts. Transfer to a gratin dish with a capacity of about 4 cups/960 ml, sprinkle the remaining cheddar on top, and bake for 15 to 20 minutes, or until the cheese on top is lightly browned and crispy. Serve hot right out of the oven.

— CIDER VINEGAR SLAW —

I hate sugary slaw, but I have to admit that a sweet note in a vinegary slaw goes with hot sauce and ribs the way rainbow jimmies go with vanilla soft-serve. There's no sugar here, but there is a whole apple in the dressing, which tastes better than sugar, delivering freshness, flavor, and sweetness. Don't skimp on the black pepper—it's essential.

1 MEDIUM HEAD WHITE CABBAGE, CORED AND SHREDDED

1 TART APPLE (JONAGOLD, PINK LADY, OR GRANNY SMITH), PEEL ON, CORED AND QUARTERED

1 SHALLOT, SLICED

1 TBSP BROWN OR DIJON MUSTARD

1/2 CUP/120 ML ORGANIC REFINED OLIVE OIL (SEE OLIVE OIL, PAGE 18)

1/2 CUP/120 ML CIDER VINEGAR

KOSHER SALT

1 TBSP CELERY SEED

BLACK PEPPER

Put the shredded cabbage in a large serving bowl. Combine the apple, shallot, mustard, olive oil, vinegar, and 1 tbsp salt in a food processor or blender and work until smooth. I prefer to dress slaw just before serving because the cabbage leaches out water once salted, diluting the dressing. When you're close to sitting down at the table, pour roughly 1/2 cup/120 ml of the dressing over the cabbage, add the celery seed, plenty of black pepper, and mix well. Taste, adding dressing, salt, or black pepper, as you like.

SPICE-BUSH OVEN BABY BACK RIBS,
ROASTED WATERMELON RADISHES, AND WILD MUSHROOMS WITH BARLEY

SERVES 4

Ribs are like theater: When they're good, they're a singular pleasure, and when they're bad, they're an embarrassment to all involved. Making stage-worthy ribs isn't all that hard, I promise. These are a simple version, neither very dry nor "wet." They achieve a perfection that settles me lower in my seat, as I add just one more contribution to the mounting pile in the bone dish.

— SPICE-BUSH OVEN BABY BACK RIBS —

¼ CUP/60 G KOSHER SALT

3 TBSP BLACK PEPPERCORNS, GROUND

3 TBSP DRY MUSTARD

3 TBSP PAPRIKA

2 TBSP SMOKED PAPRIKA

1 TBSP CAYENNE PEPPER

1 TBSP CORIANDER SEED, GROUND

1 TBSP CUMIN SEED, GROUND

4 TO 5 LB/1.8 TO 2.3 KG BABY BACK RIBS (2 OR 3 SLABS); SILVERSKIN REMOVED (SEE THE INSTRUCTIONS ON PAGE 15)

1 TBSP ORGANIC HIGH-HEAT OIL (SEE HIGH-TEMPERATURE COOKING OILS, PAGE 17)

YOUR FAVORITE HOT SAUCE FOR SERVING

Combine the salt, ground peppercorns, mustard, paprika, smoked paprika, cayenne, ground coriander seed, and ground cumin seed in a jar. Shake or stir thoroughly. You'll have about 1¼ cups/175 g. (Although you'll be using just a fraction of the rub for this recipe, you can keep it on hand in a tightly sealed jar for the next time a rib craving strikes, or rub a handful on chicken thighs or wings before grilling.)

Preheat the oven to 225°F/110°C. Rub the ribs all over with the oil and then coat with about ¼ cup/35 g rub. Set the ribs in a roasting pan, meaty-side up, and put them in the oven. Cook the ribs for 1½ hours, and then flip them over and cook for another hour or so, depending on how thick they are. They should be falling-apart tender and well browned and crispy. If the ribs aren't tender, return them to the oven for another 30 minutes and test again, but beware of drying them out. Serve with your favorite hot sauce.

— ROASTED WATERMELON RADISHES —

An unrepentant raw-radish fanatic, I roasted a bunch of these late-fall pretties because they were way too spicy for even my hearty palate. Sliced into rounds, top to bottom, they're gorgeous. Tossed with oil and roasted until they wrinkle, they're revelatory.

24 WATERMELON RADISHES, TRIMMED AND CUT INTO ¼-IN/6-MM ROUNDS (SUBSTITUTE CHERRY BELLE OR FRENCH BREAKFAST RADISHES OR ANY OTHER VARIETY YOU LIKE)

2 TBSP BEST OLIVE OIL (SEE OLIVE OIL, PAGE 18)

COARSE OR FLAKY SALT

Preheat the oven to 400°F/200°C. In a medium mixing bowl, toss the radishes with the olive oil. Spread out the radishes in a single layer on a baking sheet and roast for 8 to 10 minutes, or until they begin to shrink and the edges brown slightly. Sprinkle with salt while hot and serve.

— WILD MUSHROOMS WITH BARLEY —

If you have a source for wild mushrooms, this recipe will put
them to excellent use. Cheese and garlic enhance the flavor
of any mushroom, and the barley is a relatively neutral,
pleasantly nutty accompaniment.

1 CUP/170 G PEARLED BARLEY	3 GARLIC CLOVES, COARSELY CHOPPED
4 TBSP/55 G BUTTER	1 CUP/115 G GRATED PECORINO ROMANO
1 LB/455 G MIXED WILD MUSHROOMS (SUBSTITUTE FARMED MUSHROOMS SUCH AS MAITAKE, SHIITAKE, OR PORTOBELLO)	FLAKY SALT AND BLACK PEPPER

Bring a large pot of water to boil over high heat and add the
barley. Cook for 18 to 20 minutes, or until tender. Drain, shake dry,
and return to the pot.

While the barley cooks, melt 2 tbsp of the butter in a large sauté
pan over high heat. Add the mushrooms and cook for 5 minutes, stirring frequently. Add the garlic and cook for another 5 to 7 minutes,
or until the mushrooms have cooked off their liquid and begin to
smell toasty.

Stir the remaining 2 tbsp butter into the warm barley, along with
the cheese.

Add the mushrooms, a pinch of flaky salt, and a grind of black
pepper to the barley. Taste for seasoning and serve.

BBQ RIBS WITH SPICY MOP,
PICKLED ONION SLAW, AND DEVILED EGGS WITH DEBRIS

SERVES 4

People get worked up over how to cook ribs, and for good reason. Everyone seems to have a secret to "the best" rub, mop, or sauce. I don't really buy into the voodoo of it all. Besides, I don't like my ribs overwhelmed by sauce or spice. Happy, healthy pigs produce delicious ribs if the meat is cooked long, slow, and smoky. Whatever you do or don't put on them, the fatty, crispy deliciousness of gnawing tender meat off a bone can't be denied.

The name of the sauce comes, obviously enough, from the doll-size janitor mops that pit masters use to coat their meat. A mop helps to keep the meat moist while giving it a little extra flavor over the course of its long, slow cooking. Get a real string mop to apply this sauce—they're much more efficient than the more common silicone type, and cute to boot. You will need 5 handfuls hardwood chips, soaked for at least 30 minutes in water and drained, for smoking the ribs.

— BBQ RIBS WITH SPICY MOP —

4 TO 5 LB/1.8 TO 2.3 KG ST. LOUIS-CUT RIBS OR SPARERIBS (2 OR 3 SLABS), SILVERSKIN REMOVED (SEE THE INSTRUCTIONS ON PAGE 15)

1 TSP KOSHER SALT

BLACK PEPPER

ABOUT 1 TBSP ORGANIC HIGH-HEAT OIL
(SEE HIGH-TEMPERATURE COOKING OILS, PAGE 17)

SPICY MOP
¼ CUP/60 ML WORCESTERSHIRE SAUCE

¼ CUP/50 G BROWN SUGAR (DARK OR LIGHT)

1 CUP/240 ML CIDER VINEGAR

2 TBSP PEANUT OR VEGETABLE OIL

2 TBSP HOT SAUCE

1 TBSP SMOKED PAPRIKA

FLAKY SALT (OPTIONAL)

HOT SAUCE FOR SERVING

Build a medium fire in a charcoal or wood grill or heat a gas grill to medium. If you're using charcoal or wood, you want hot embers, not flames. (If you don't have a grill large enough to place the meat away from the heat source, make a small fire or set the grill to its lowest setting.) Use a clean, well-cured grate. Place a handful of wood chips on the fire. Repeat every hour, adding charcoal or wood and wood chips to maintain the smoke and a steady temperature. Add fuel more frequently if the temperature dips to below 200°F/95 C. It should hover between 200 and 350°F/95 and 180°C.

Rinse the ribs if they've been in a vacuum pack. Either way, dry them and then rub all over with the kosher salt and a sprinkling of black pepper. Rub on a light gloss of oil.

Place the ribs a few inches/centimetres away from the heat source if possible. Cover the grill, and smoke for 3 to 3½ hours.

When the ribs are on the grill, make the Spicy Mop: Whisk together the Worcestershire, brown sugar, cider vinegar, peanut oil, hot sauce, and smoked paprika in a small saucepan and set over medium heat until the liquid comes to a boil. Pouring off ¾ cup/180 ml into a separate container, cover, and reserve to season the pork once it's cooked. Keep the remaining mop hot inside the covered grill as you use it to coat the meat during cooking. This will concentrate it and fuse the flavors, while killing off any bacteria you may introduce from the uncooked meat. (If the mop reduces too far, add a splash of your open beer—or wine, or water—to the pot.)

Every hour mop the ribs, turn the meat over, and mop the side now facing up. The ribs are done when you can slip a bone out of the rack and it comes out nearly clean. Taste the ribs for salt, and if they could use a little more, sprinkle with flaky salt. Serve with extra mop and more hot sauce on the side.

— PICKLED ONION SLAW —

As you may have noticed, I don't do raw onions. Shallots, yes;
onions, no. This is as close as I get, but I do throw these pickled
onions around my recipes the way I throw around black pepper.
They're versatile and provide a reliable hit of acidity and spice
along with a subtle hint of mustard.

1 SMALL HEAD RED OR GREEN CABBAGE
(OR A COMBINATION), CORED AND
SHREDDED OR CHOPPED

1 CUP/170 G PICKLED ONIONS (PAGE 201),
CHOPPED, PLUS ¾ CUP/180 ML OF THE
PICKLED ONION BRINE

2 TBSP HONEY

¼ CUP/60 ML ORGANIC REFINED OLIVE OIL
(SEE OLIVE OIL, PAGE 18)

½ TSP KOSHER SALT

BLACK PEPPER

FLAKY SALT (OPTIONAL)

Combine the cabbage and pickled onions in a mixing bowl. In
a small saucepan, combine the brine, honey, olive oil, kosher
salt, and plenty of black pepper. Heat just until the honey
dissolves. Allow to cool briefly before mixing into the cabbage.
Before serving, dress the slaw (and no sooner, to avoid soggy,
watered-down slaw) and taste, adding a pinch of flaky salt (or
a little more brine), as you like.

— DEVILED EGGS WITH DEBRIS —

If you ever crave some truly outstanding barbecued beef brisket, hit up Mighty Quinn's at the Stockton Market in Stockton, New Jersey. On the menu alongside the best brisket I've ever tasted, they offer Deviled Eggs with Debris, which, as they explained to me, means deviled eggs sprinkled with bits of crispy exterior from barbecued pork. I think these babies deserve a place in the vernacular, so here's my version and my homage to the Mighty Quinn. It's best to make deviled eggs just before serving, as they cannot be left at room temperature, and when refrigerated, they tend to sweat as they warm up. As lovely as day-old eggs are, peeling very fresh eggs that have been hard-boiled is tedious work; eggs that are a week old or more will peel more easily.

3 DOZEN EGGS

2 CUPS/480 ML MAYONNAISE

1 TBSP DRY MUSTARD

1/4 TSP CAYENNE PEPPER

1/4 CUP/10 G SNIPPED FRESH CHIVES

PAPRIKA FOR SPRINKLING

1/2 CUP/120 ML PACKED CHOPPED PORK DEBRIS (THE MEAT FROM 1 WHOLE RIB OR THE CRISPY EXTERIOR FROM COOKED SHOULDER OR BELLY)

FLAKY SALT AND BLACK PEPPER FOR FINISHING

Bring a large pot of water to a boil over high heat. Lower the eggs into the water gently and boil for 12 minutes. Drain and run cold water over the cooked eggs until they are cool, 2 to 3 minutes. After cooling the eggs in cold water, leave them in the pot as you work, knocking them against the side of the pot before you begin to peel each one. This helps the shells come away more easily.

Halve the white lengthwise, split the egg apart, remove the yolk, and place the two halves of cooked white on a large platter or tray. As you work, collect the yolks in the bowl of a stand mixer (or in a mixing bowl if you have a hand mixer). Add the mayonnaise, dry mustard, and cayenne to the bowl with the yolks. Using the paddle attachment, beat the yolks for 2 to 3 minutes or until very smooth and fluffy.

Stuff the yolk mixture into a pastry bag fitted with a wide tip (decorative is fine, but a fine tip will quickly clog). Fill the whites with the yolk mixture, using it all. Sprinkle the deviled eggs with chives, a tiny pinch of paprika, a bit of the debris, and a pinch of flaky salt. Finish with black pepper and serve.

CAROLINA PULLED PORK SANDWICH
WITH MUSTARD SAUCE, PEG'S COLD POTATOES, AND CRISP BEAN SALAD

SERVES 4

As a Northeastern girl, I'm certainly not going to put myself in the middle of the North-versus-South Carolina food fight over the best way to make a pulled pork sandwich. (This one is my favorite—I'm sure yours is great, too. Really.) By tradition, this one happens to be more in the style of South Carolina. There's definitely no tomato involved and the predominant flavor, beyond vinegar, is mustard. You can make pulled pork from pork shoulder, of course, but your meat won't be quite as decadent and succulent as pulled belly. If you do use a shoulder, just pull and toss with a little more sauce, maybe even adding 2 or 3 tbsp of melted butter to the mix if it seems a little dry. You will need 5 handfuls wood chips, soaked for at least 30 minutes in water and drained, for smoking the belly.

— CAROLINA PULLED PORK SANDWICH —

2 SLABS PORK BELLY, ABOUT 2 IN/5 CM THICK
(FOR A TOTAL OF 8 TO 10 LB/3.6 TO 4.5 KG)

2 TBSP KOSHER SALT

2 TBSP BROWN SUGAR (DARK OR LIGHT)

2 TBSP SMOKED PAPRIKA

1 TSP CAYENNE PEPPER

2 TBSP BLACK PEPPER

MUSTARD SAUCE (PAGE 53)

6 TO 8 SOFT BUNS OR 12 TO 16 MINIBUNS

Take the meat out of the refrigerator, dry it, and let it rest to take the chill off while you prepare the fire. Mix together the salt, brown sugar, paprika, cayenne, and black pepper in a small bowl to make the rub.

Build a medium fire in a charcoal or wood grill or a smoker, or heat a gas grill to medium. Use a clean, well-cured grate. Place a handful of wood chips on the fire. Repeat every hour, adding more charcoal or wood and wood chips to maintain the smoke and a steady temperature. Add fuel more frequently if the temperature dips below 200°F/95°C. It should hover between 200 and 300°F/95 and 150°C.

Coat the meat on both sides with the rub, and then use butcher's string to tie the two sides of belly together so that the skin on each faces out. (If there's no skin, face the fattiest side out.)

When your charcoal has burned down enough to white ash-coated coals, scatter a handful of wood chips over the fire. Place the meat over indirect heat in your smoker or grill. (In other words, do not put it over the fire but next to it and well enough away so as not to burn.) Close the lid on the grill and cook for 1 hour. Turn the meat over and continue to cook for 6 to 8 hours, checking each hour. How long the meat will take to cook depends on its size and thickness, the temperature of the fire, and even the temperature outdoors. When the meat is crusty brown on the outside and extremely tender, it's done. Test it after 6 hours by pulling off a piece and popping it in your mouth.

Remove the meat from the grill and let it cool enough to handle before pulling it. (You can use heat-proof gloves to speed things up.) To pull the meat, use a fork or your hands to rip the meat into threads. Don't chop it—although you can chop the skin into small bits since it may be quite tough. Just try not to get rid of any of that crusty exterior, if you can help it. Toss with the mustard sauce until well seasoned, and serve on the buns.

— MUSTARD SAUCE —

After you pull the pork, you'll toss it with this sauce to give it
a tangy, sweet-and-spicy mustard-and-vinegar flavor. The sauce
also moistens the meat, and you want the pork—already succulent—
to be fabulously moist.

1 TBSP WORCESTERSHIRE SAUCE

2 TBSP BROWN SUGAR (DARK OR LIGHT)

1/2 CUP/120 ML CIDER VINEGAR

1/2 CUP/120 ML MUSTARD (DIJON, YELLOW,
OR BROWN MUSTARD WILL WORK;
AVOID GRAINY MUSTARD)

2 TBSP HOT SAUCE

1 TSP KOSHER SALT

BLACK PEPPER

In a small saucepan set over low heat, combine the Worcestershire,
brown sugar, vinegar, mustard, hot sauce, salt, and a good grind of
black pepper. Bring to a simmer and cook gently for 10 to 12 minutes. Set aside until ready to use. Reheat the sauce, if necessary,
so that it's hot when it goes on the pork.

— PEG'S COLD POTATOES —

My maternal grandmother, Peg, short for Marguerite, was a truly impressive woman, but nobody would accuse her of being a cook. The single edible item she'd mastered was a robust potato salad. Maybe it was her Irish blood? This is the taste I remember from many picnics we spent gazing out through the humid air at the smudged swimmers and sailboats crowding Long Island Sound.

2 LB/910 G RED POTATOES, NOT PEELED

4 EGGS, HARD-BOILED, PEELED, AND SLICED

1/2 TSP DRY MUSTARD

1/2 TO 3/4 CUP/120 TO 180 ML MAYONNAISE

1/4 CUP/10 G SNIPPED FRESH CHIVES

1 TSP KOSHER SALT

BLACK PEPPER

Put the potatoes in a large saucepan, cover with water, and set over high heat. Bring the water to a boil and cook the potatoes for 20 to 25 minutes, or until the potatoes are tender—not falling apart. Drain and then run under cold water to cool.

Dice the potatoes into bite-size chunks and put them in a mixing bowl. Add the eggs, mustard, mayonnaise, half the chives, the salt, and a few grinds of pepper. Mix well, taste for seasoning, and serve with the remaining chives sprinkled on top.

— CRISP BEAN SALAD —

Forget all the mushy bean salads you've eaten. This one is fresh and crunchy—thanks to plenty of celery, herbs, and tomato. The beans are a smooth, rich addition rather than a monotonous filler.

ONE 15-OZ/430-G CAN CANNELLINI BEANS, DRAINED AND RINSED

1/4 CUP/10 G CHOPPED FRESH PARSLEY

2 TBSP FRESH THYME LEAVES

1 TOMATO, DICED

1 SHALLOT, CHOPPED

2 RIBS CELERY, THINLY SLICED

2 TBSP BEST OLIVE OIL (SEE OLIVE OIL, PAGE 18)

1 TBSP CIDER VINEGAR

1/2 TSP KOSHER SALT

Combine the cannellini beans, parsley, thyme, tomato, shallot, celery, olive oil, vinegar, and salt in a large bowl. Mix well and serve.

BACON-SWADDLED MEAT LOAF
WITH TWICE-BAKED POTATOES AND BLUE CHEESE–ICEBERG WEDGE

SERVES 4

One of the earliest known cookbooks, Apicius's *Cooking and Dining in Imperial Rome*, likely offers the first recipe for what we call meat loaf. Called forcemeat, it contained myrtle berries, crushed nuts, and pepper. The meat—pork it seems, although it is not specified in the original—was held together by finely ground "hearts of wheat," diluted in wine. The whole was shaped into small rolls and wrapped in caul. My version is more conventional—wrapped in bacon, not caulfat, and made with veal and beef as well as pork. I'm extraordinarily picky about my meat loaf; I think you'll find this one exceptional. Don't forget the cold meat loaf sandwich, which I'm convinced all men eat with a whopping slice of raw onion.

— BACON-SWADDLED MEAT LOAF —

1 LB/455 G GROUND PORK

1 LB/455 G GROUND VEAL

1 LB/455 G GROUND BEEF, 80% LEAN

1 TBSP BUTTER

1 RED ONION, FINELY CHOPPED

1/4 CUP/50 G FINELY CHOPPED SHALLOT

1 TBSP SRIRACHA OR ANOTHER HOT SAUCE

2 TBSP DRY MUSTARD

1 TSP KOSHER SALT

1/2 TSP BLACK PEPPER

2 TBSP WORCESTERSHIRE SAUCE

2 EGGS

1/2 CUP/120 ML SOUR CREAM

1/2 CUP/50 G MATZOH MEAL OR SUPERFINE BREAD CRUMBS

1/2 CUP/20 G CHOPPED FRESH PARSLEY

2 TBSP FRESH THYME LEAVES

12 PIECES BACON

SLICED RAW ONION FOR SERVING

KETCHUP FOR SERVING

Remove the pork, veal, and beef from the refrigerator and set it out to take the chill off for 30 minutes before baking. Position a rack in the middle or lower third of the oven and preheat the oven to 350°F/180°C. Melt the butter in a medium frying pan set over medium heat. When it's bubbling, add the red onion and cook for 5 to 8 minutes, or until soft and lightly colored. Transfer to a small bowl to cool. In a large mixing bowl, whisk together the shallot, Sriracha, dry mustard, salt, pepper, Worcestershire, eggs, and sour cream. Add the pork, veal, and beef and mix until just combined. (I use my hands for this job.) Add the matzoh meal, parsley, and thyme and mix until just combined.

Line a baking sheet with parchment or aluminum foil. Dump the meat onto the baking sheet and use your hands to shape it into a humped rectangle. The loaf should be wide enough that when a piece of bacon is stretched across it, the ends are just long enough to tuck under the edges of the loaf. It need not be exact. When the loaf is shaped, swaddle it in bacon. Begin at one end, laying a strip across the loaf and tucking the ends under it. Lay the next one overlapping the first by a third of its width. You will use 10 to 12 strips of bacon.

Place the meat loaf in the oven and cook until an instant-read thermometer inserted into the center of the loaf reaches 165°F/74°C. Begin checking after 1 hour, and if it's not ready, cook for an additional 10 to 15 minutes before testing again. Once the meat loaf is done, allow it to rest for 10 minutes before cutting into generous 1-in/2.5-cm slices. Serve with slices of raw onion and ketchup.

— TWICE-BAKED POTATOES —

Retro, bordering on ironic, the twice-baked potato earns its place
on the table through sheer decadence. If you're old enough, the
taste may make you nostalgic; if you're not, the taste may make you
a believer.

2 LARGE BAKING POTATOES, PREFERABLY
IDAHO RUSSETS

1 TBSP PEANUT OR VEGETABLE OIL

1/2 CUP/120 ML SOUR CREAM

1/2 CUP/120 ML HEAVY CREAM

1/2 TSP KOSHER SALT

BLACK PEPPER

6 GREEN ONIONS, WHITE AND TENDER GREEN PARTS
ONLY, SLICED

1 CUP/115 G GRATED SHARP CHEDDAR CHEESE

1/4 CUP/10 G SNIPPED FRESH CHIVES

Preheat the oven to 350°F/180°C. Thoroughly wash and dry the potatoes. Rub all over with peanut oil and puncture the skin in several
spots with a fork. Place on the oven rack and bake for 45 to 55 minutes, or until tender. Insert a paring knife into the center of a
potato to test for resistance; if it slides right in, the potato is
done. Remove the potatoes from the oven, but leave the oven on.
Cut the potatoes in half lengthwise.

Gently scoop the flesh out into a medium bowl, working carefully so
as not to rip or puncture the skin. Press the potato flesh through
a ricer into a mixing bowl.

In a small saucepan, whisk together the sour cream, heavy cream,
salt, and a grind of pepper. Place over medium heat and watch carefully. It should get very hot but not boil. Pour the hot cream over
the potato flesh, add the green onions and 3/4 cup/85 g of the cheddar, and stir until just combined. Don't overwork. Spoon the potato
mixture back into the potato skins, sprinkle with the remaining
1/4 cup/30 g cheese, and bake for 10 to 12 minutes, or until the
cheese is melted. (You can use a broiler if you prefer.) Sprinkle
with the fresh chives and serve.

— BLUE CHEESE—ICEBERG WEDGE —

Another retro favorite, this one has seen a trendy resurgence of late, because nobody can seem to resist the crispy appeal of iceberg lettuce (so unlike all the tender baby greens we eat these days) paired with potent blue cheese. The whole is brought to indulgent heights when topped with fatty, salty bacon bits. If you prefer, this recipe made with more flavorful but still crispy romaine is also excellent. Ruthlessly discard any tough outer leaves.

1 CUP/240 ML MAYONNAISE

¼ CUP/60 ML BUTTERMILK (SUBSTITUTE WHOLE MILK WITH A SQUEEZE OF LEMON)

¼ CUP/60 ML SOUR CREAM

JUICE OF ½ LEMON

7 OZ/200 G BLUE CHEESE, CRUMBLED INTO SMALL PIECES

1 LARGE HEAD ICEBERG LETTUCE OR 2 HEADS ROMAINE, HALVED TOP TO BOTTOM

¼ CUP/10 G SNIPPED FRESH CHIVES

BLACK PEPPER

2 OZ/55 G BACON, COOKED UNTIL CRISP AND CRUMBLED

In a small mixing bowl, thoroughly mix together the mayonnaise, buttermilk, sour cream, lemon juice, and cheese. Place the iceberg lettuce on a platter and pour the dressing over the cut surface, splitting it between the halves. Allow the dressing to seep into the spaces between the tightly packed leaves for 5 to 10 minutes. Cut each lettuce half in half again. Place each iceberg quarter or two romaine quarters on a plate. Scrape any remaining dressing from the platter into a small bowl and distribute it among the quarters. (You may or may not want to use all the dressing, depending on the size of your head of lettuce.) Sprinkle with the chives, grind a good bit of black pepper over each portion, and scatter with bacon bits to finish before serving.

FENNEL HASH WITH POACHED EGG,
MOLASSES CORN BREAD, AND BRAISED DANDELION GREENS

SERVES 4

Although hash is most familiar in its venerable canned form, the canned can't compare with the fresh, authentic version. The staple of many a "kids' meal" growing up, I loved hash—can or no can. It is one of the few foods I eat with ketchup (burgers and meat loaf are the others). Hash made with pork and fennel, instead of starchy potatoes, is not to be missed. Paired with the slightly bitter note of dandelion greens and a hunk of corn bread, this meal puts me in mind of breakfast for dinner, without taking that worthwhile instinct too far.

— FENNEL HASH WITH POACHED EGG —

1 LB/455 G GROUND PORK

2 TBSP BUTTER

1 SWEET ONION, SUCH AS VIDALIA, CHOPPED

5 RIBS CELERY, CHOPPED

2 FENNEL BULBS, DICED

1/2 CUP/20 G CHOPPED FRESH PARSLEY

1/4 TSP PAPRIKA

PINCH OF CAYENNE PEPPER

1 TSP FENNEL SEED

BLACK PEPPER

KOSHER SALT

4 EGGS, FRIED OR POACHED, YOLK RUNNY

FLAKY SALT FOR FINISHING

KETCHUP FOR SERVING

HOT SAUCE FOR SERVING (OPTIONAL)

Brown the pork in a large sauté pan set over high heat, stirring frequently, 10 to 12 minutes. Transfer to a plate and set aside. Melt the butter in the same pan (without washing it) and cook the onion for 8 to 10 minutes, or until soft. Return the meat to the pan and add the celery, diced fennel, parsley, paprika, cayenne, fennel seed, and what your judgment tells you is too much black pepper (but really isn't). Cook for 5 to 8 minutes, or until the fennel and celery are beginning to soften and lose their raw flavor. Add ½ tsp kosher salt and taste, adding more as needed.

Portion the hash out, top each serving with an egg, and give the egg a good pinch of flaky salt. Serve with ketchup and maybe a tiny bit of hot sauce.

— MOLASSES CORN BREAD —

Made dark and moist with blackstrap molasses, this hearty corn bread takes nicely to the earthy flavors of this meal. Blackstrap molasses is darker and less sweet than conventional dark or light molasses. I recommend it here, but any kind will work. Plenty of salted butter and a sticky drizzle of buckwheat honey never go amiss when it comes to corn bread.

1 TBSP BUTTER, PLUS ½ CUP/115 G, MELTED

½ CUP/120 ML MOLASSES, PREFERABLY BLACKSTRAP

½ CUP/120 ML MILK

2 EGGS

1½ CUPS/200 G CORNMEAL, MEDIUM OR FINE GROUND

1½ CUPS/190 G ALL-PURPOSE FLOUR

1 TSP BAKING POWDER

1 TSP BAKING SODA

½ TSP KOSHER SALT

Preheat the oven to 350°F/180°C. Put the 1 tbsp butter in a 10-in/25-cm round cast-iron frying pan. Put the frying pan in the oven to heat for 5 to 10 minutes.

In a large mixing bowl, thoroughly whisk together the ½ cup/115 g melted butter, molasses, milk, and eggs. Without mixing again until you've added all the ingredients, add the cornmeal, flour, baking powder, baking soda, and salt. Mix until just wet, leaving no dry lumps in the batter.

Take the hot frying pan out of the oven, swirl the butter around to coat the bottom, and pour in the batter, spreading it around into an even layer. Bake for 18 to 20 minutes, or until the bread begins to crack slightly and pull away from the edges of the pan. Be sure it's not raw at the center—it's difficult to tell when to take it out of the oven because one of your cues will be off—this corn bread looks dark well before it's done. Test with a toothpick—when inserted in the center it should come out clean. Let it sit for 5 minutes, cut into portions, and serve warm right out of the pan.

— BRAISED DANDELION GREENS —

This hearty, pernicious weed is tasty when thoroughly cooked. It grows in the Southern United States throughout the winter and plagues gardeners elsewhere in the summer months. It is now widely cultivated thanks to its resurgent popularity in the kitchen. You can pick your own in early spring or winter (in the South). Look for young plants with small, tender leaves, or you'll find the wild variety unbearably bitter.

1 LB/455 G DANDELION GREENS, INCLUDING STEMS

3 EXTRA-THICK SLICES BACON, CUT INTO 1-IN/2.5-CM PIECES

1 RED ONION, THINLY SLICED

2 TBSP WATER

1/2 TSP KOSHER SALT

1 TBSP CIDER VINEGAR

Cut off the bottom portion of each dandelion, which is mostly stem and extends almost halfway up the plant. Roughly chop the leaves and set aside.

Cook the bacon in a large heavy frying pan set over medium-low heat until crisp. Remove to a paper towel. Drain some fat from the pan, leaving behind 1 to 2 tbsp. Add the onion and cook over medium heat until soft, 8 to 10 minutes. Without washing the pan, add the greens. Cook for 2 to 3 minutes over medium heat, stirring frequently, until the leaves begin to brown in spots. Add the water and salt and cook for 15 to 20 minutes, or until the water has evaporated. Add the vinegar and return the onions and bacon to the pan to reheat. Serve hot.

WHOLE-YOLK RAVIOLI
OVER SLOW-COOKED PORK BELLY AND WILTED MIXED GREENS WITH BUTTERY TOAST AND SAUTÉED SECKEL PEARS

SERVES 4

If you're feeling ambitious, this recipe is a dinner party high-wire act. Unless you get your mise en place in impeccable order ahead of time, you'll miss the whole party. (Getting your mise en place in order is, of course, a fancy French way of saying you've prepared all your ingredients—measuring, chopping, blanching, and peeling—so they're ready when you need them.) While I won't pretend this isn't a challenging recipe, it's really not all *that* difficult. The showy rewards of that runny egg yolk oozing out of the ravioli to make a delicious mess on your plate are pretty spectacular. Compose each plate with the Wilted Mixed Greens on the bottom, sliced Slow-Cooked Pork Belly layered over that. Place three ravioli on top, the whole-yolk one in the center. The Sautéed Seckel Pear halves and Buttery Toast should flank on each side, toast opposite toast, pear opposite pear.

— WHOLE-YOLK RAVIOLI —

Making your own pasta is one of those kitchen tasks that daunts many cooks. Forge onward—it doesn't take an expert to get honorable results. Freshly made sheep's-milk ricotta rather than standard-issue store-bought stuff has flavor the way a tomato from your garden has flavor. Look for it—Italian markets are a good place to begin. Working with the egg yolks can be frustrating; again, high-quality eggs that are very fresh will make a difference, as the membrane will be thicker and less apt to break. *Courage!*

RAVIOLI DOUGH

2 CUPS/255 G ALL-PURPOSE FLOUR

1/2 TSP KOSHER SALT

2 EGGS

2 TBSP WATER

RAVIOLI FILLING

1/2 CUP/110 G RICOTTA CHEESE

1/4 CUP/25 G FINELY GRATED PARMESAN CHEESE (REGGIANO) OR GRANA PADANA

3 TBSP FRESH THYME LEAVES

2 TBSP ORGANIC REFINED OLIVE OIL (SEE OLIVE OIL, PAGE 18)

1/2 TSP KOSHER SALT

BLACK PEPPER

4 EGGS (PLUS EXTRA FOR INSURANCE AGAINST MISTAKES)

2 TBSP ORGANIC REFINED OLIVE OIL (SEE OLIVE OIL, PAGE 18)

PINCH OF KOSHER SALT

1 TBSP BEST OLIVE OIL (SEE OLIVE OIL, PAGE 18), OR BUTTER, MELTED

COARSE OR FLAKY SALT FOR FINISHING

To make the ravioli dough: Pour the flour onto an immaculate work surface, sprinkle the salt over the flour, and make a well in the center. Crack the eggs into the well and use the tips of your fingers to begin mixing the flour with the eggs. Once the eggs are loosely incorporated into the flour, you'll have a rough, dry mix that is not even close to forming a ball of dough. Make another well in the center and add the water, slowly incorporating it into the dough. Begin to knead the dough by pressing it with your palms. Use the rough ball that forms to collect stray bits of flour and egg not yet incorporated. Eventually you will have a coarse, blotchy ball that you can knead more easily. Work this dough for about 15 minutes. It will be very tough at first but will become smoother and more workable as the gluten develops. If you find the dough much too tough to knead at all, wet your hands and continue working the dough. That extra bit of water should help. Once you have a smooth, almost glossy ball, wrap it tightly in plastic wrap, press it into a disk with your palm, and place it on the counter to rest for 1 hour.

Meanwhile, make the ravioli filling: In a small mixing bowl, combine the ricotta, Parmesan, thyme, refined olive oil, kosher salt, and pepper. Mix thoroughly, cover with plastic wrap, and set aside.

Unwrap the dough after it has rested, place it on a clean work surface, and cut it into quarters. Press one with your hand to flatten it slightly and set a pasta machine on its thickest setting. Work the pasta dough through several times, setting the roller thinner and thinner each time. (The less pressure each time, the better; notch down gradually.) Your aim is extremely thin dough, but dough that you can still handle and work with. Lightly flour your work surface and use a 2½-in/6-cm round cutter to cut out circles from the dough. You should have six rounds. Repeat the rolling and cutting process with the remaining three pieces of dough to make twenty-four rounds (which will produce four egg-and-ricotta-filled ravioli and eight simple ricotta-filled ravioli). Cover with a damp towel until ready to use to prevent the dough from drying and cracking. (Alternatively, cut the ravioli out as you fill them, keeping the quarters of dough tightly sealed in plastic wrap.)

Line a baking sheet with parchment paper and flour it lightly. Dab about 1 tsp ricotta filling in the center of a round of pasta dough. Spread it out to create a little crater for an egg yolk to sit in. Using your bare hands, crack and separate an egg, setting the yolk on the filling very gently so it doesn't slide off. Take another round for the top, pulling it gently on the edges to stretch it ever so slightly before setting it on top of the yolk. Working slowly and carefully, crimp the edges tightly together. Watch that the yolk remains centered as you work. (You will almost certainly break one. Don't worry. Just throw the whole thing out, clean your work surface, and start again.) Lay each completed ravioli on the baking sheet. Repeat until you have four perfect ravioli. (You could make an extra as insurance against breakage if you like.) Repeat the process with-out the egg yolks for the remaining ravioli, making a total of eight plain ones. Finally, be sure to find a way to distinguish between the egg and plain ravioli—I crimp the edges of my plain ravioli, so that I can see what's what when they come out of the water.

Fill a large stockpot with cold water and bring it to a boil. Add the 2 tbsp refined olive oil to the water along with the pinch of kosher salt. Carefully add the ravioli to the pot. Once all the ravioli are in the pot, use a thin metal spatula to gently nudge the pasta from the bottom of the pot. (They really will stick!) Within 2 to 3 minutes, the ravioli should rise to the surface. Once they do, remove them from the pot with a slotted spoon and place them directly on warm plates, making sure to distribute the whole-yolk ravioli equally. Drizzle the ravioli with the best olive oil. Serve quickly, with just a pinch of coarse salt, as the yolk will continue to cook.

— SLOW-COOKED PORK BELLY —

This is my basic belly-cooking method. I like it because it never fails me, and I don't have to do anything more than rub on a little salt and pepper and stick the meat in the oven. The biggest component of this recipe is time; so long as you have plenty of that, you can't disgrace yourself.

2 TO 4 LB/910 G TO 1.8 KG PORK BELLY

1 TO 2 TSP KOSHER SALT

BLACK PEPPER

Preheat the oven to 200°F/95°C. Coat the belly with the salt and a few grinds of pepper on both sides. (Use more or less salt, according to the size of the meat.) Place in a large cast-iron frying pan, skin-side up, and roast for 4 to 5 hours. The meat should be extremely tender and the fat soft.

Slice as thinly as possible. You will not use all the belly for the ravioli plates, although you may end up bringing the leftovers to the table for those who can't resist a bite or two more. Don't be surprised if it all disappears—I've never managed to have any left over for a midnight snack.

— WILTED MIXED GREENS —

Whenever you need a quick side, this is one of the fastest, easiest, and most healthful recipes to throw together.

2 TBSP ORGANIC REFINED OLIVE OIL
(SEE OLIVE OIL, PAGE 18)

1 LB/455 G MIXED BABY COLLARDS, KALE, CHARD, AND SPINACH, OR IN ANY COMBINATION YOU LIKE

½ TSP KOSHER SALT

1 TBSP WHITE WINE OR CHAMPAGNE VINEGAR

Heat the olive oil in a large sauté pan set over medium heat until just simmering before adding the greens, salt, and vinegar. Cook, using tongs to turn the greens, for 3 to 4 minutes, or until just wilted. Transfer to warm plates, spreading the greens out in the center of the plate.

— BUTTERY TOAST —

This is not a recipe. It's buttery toast made from the best bread and
the best butter you can lay your hands on. Think cultured butter
and sour, chewy levain from a French-trained baker.

4 SLICES LEVAIN OR *PAIN DE SEIGLE*   2 TBSP SALTED BUTTER

Toast the bread, and butter it generously. (Alternatively, toast the
bread ahead of time and keep it warm in the oven.) Cut each slice in
half before placing the bread on plates.

— SAUTÉED SECKEL PEARS —

Seckel pears are small and pretty, but you should use what you
can find. Ripe but firm is what you want. The pears will darken as
they cook, so the Seckels' appealing, pretty skin is lost. If you use
a larger pear, consider cooking just 2 pears. Then again, there's
nothing more tasty than an extra bite of that salty, fatty pork
belly with the soft, buttery, sweet pear.

4 SECKEL PEARS, RIPE BUT STILL FIRM   2 TBSP COGNAC
            2 TBSP BUTTER

Cut the pears in half lengthwise, leaving the pretty stem on one
half. Use a 1-tsp measure or a melon baller to scoop out the center,
removing the seeds. Combine the butter and cognac in a large sauté
pan set over very low heat. When the butter is melted, add the pears,
cut-side down. Cook for 25 to 30 minutes, or until the pears are
soft and the skin has darkened. The cut side of the pear should
be lightly browned. Keep the pears warm in the oven until ready
to serve.

PIG PIZZA

SERVES 4

Pizza may be a vehicle for ingredients or a means of worshipping crust with just a taste of cheese and sauce. This pizza does both—crust, sauce, and cheese loaded with toppings, as if a greedy five-year-old got carried away with the takeout menu at the local pizza joint. It's a decadent carnival of textures and flavors. Don't cheat along the way—the quality of every component counts. Although if you aren't up to making your own dough, buy it from the best pizza joint you know. Ask for one 1½-lb/680-g disk of dough or enough for a large pie.

The keys to the fresh sauce are local tomatoes grown for their flavor in rich dirt at the height of summer tomato season. Don't bother with jarred sauce. In winter use the best cherry tomatoes you can buy and add a pinch or two of sugar to the sauce.

PIZZA DOUGH

1½ CUPS/360 ML WARM (NOT HOT) WATER

1 TSP INSTANT YEAST

1 TBSP KOSHER SALT

1 TSP SUGAR

¼ CUP/60 ML EXTRA-VIRGIN OLIVE OIL
(SEE OLIVE OIL, PAGE 18)

2 TBSP CHOPPED FRESH ROSEMARY

3½ CUPS/440 G UNBLEACHED ALL-PURPOSE FLOUR

FRESH TOMATO SAUCE

2 LB/910 G CHERRY TOMATOES, PUNCTURED

1 TSP KOSHER SALT

3 TBSP ORGANIC REFINED OLIVE OIL
(SEE OLIVE OIL, PAGE 18)

½ HEAD GARLIC, CLOVES CRUSHED, PEELED,
AND COARSELY SLICED

1 TSP RED WINE VINEGAR (OPTIONAL)

6 TBSP/90 ML ORGANIC REFINED OLIVE OIL
(SEE OLIVE OIL, PAGE 18)

1 VIDALIA ONION, VERY THINLY SLICED

1½ LB/680 G FRESHLY MADE MOZZARELLA CHEESE,
SLICED AND DRAINED, AS NEEDED

½ YELLOW BELL PEPPER, VERY THINLY SLICED

1 TBSP FENNEL SEED, CRUSHED

8 OZ/225 G THICK-SLICED BACON, CUBED AND
COOKED UNTIL JUST CRISP

GENEROUS 1 HANDFUL FRESH BABY
SPINACH LEAVES

FLAKY OR COARSE SALT

1 TBSP CHOPPED FRESH OREGANO

½ CUP/20 G FRESH BASIL LEAVES,
SNIPPED INTO THREADS

To make the pizza dough: Mix the water, yeast, kosher salt, and sugar together in the bowl of a stand mixer or in a mixing bowl, if working by hand. Add the olive oil, rosemary, and flour. If using a stand mixer, attach a dough hook and work at medium speed for 5 minutes. If working by hand, use a wooden spoon to mix the dough and then turn out onto a clean, lightly floured surface. Oil your hands and work the dough, kneading until you have a cohesive ball of elastic dough. Whichever method you use, oil your hands, coat the dough, and place in a well-oiled bowl to rise at room temperature for 1 to 2 hours.

While the dough is rising, make the tomato sauce: Combine the tomatoes, salt, olive oil, and garlic in a large sauté pan set over medium-low heat. Cook, stirring frequently with a heat-proof rubber spatula, for 20 to 25 minutes. The sauce should be almost the consistency of tomato paste, or so thick that you can scrape your spatula down the center of the pan, and the line you make will remain there. Set the sauce aside. It will thicken as it cools, which is just fine. When you're ready to make the pizza, stir in the vinegar (if using). Fresh is fresh, so it's best not to work ahead, but if you have leftovers, the sauce will keep, refrigerated, for 3 or 4 days.

Preheat the oven to 500°F/260°C. Heat 2 tbsp of the refined olive oil in a sauté pan set over low heat and add the onion. Cook very slowly, stirring frequently, for 20 to 25 minutes, or until the onion is a golden, sticky mass. Set aside.

Coat a baking sheet with a generous gloss of oil and set aside. Cover an immaculate surface with a dusting of flour and roll out the dough in a shape that approximates your baking sheet. If you have a rimless baking sheet, transfer the partially rolled dough to the baking sheet and roll it until it's very thin and fully covers the surface. If your baking sheet is rimmed, continue rolling until the dough is thin, and then transfer by folding the dough over on itself and laying it flat once it's on the baking sheet. Using a pastry brush or your hands, coat the top of the dough with the remaining 4 tbsp/60 ml refined olive oil. Lay the sliced mozzarella over the dough evenly, along with the bell pepper and caramelized onions. Scatter the fennel seed over the top. Using a spoon, place 1 cup/240 ml of the sauce in strategic spots, without covering the whole surface of the dough (you won't use all the sauce). It can and should cover some of the cheese and toppings. Scatter on the bacon and spinach.

Bake for 15 to 20 minutes, or until the edge is beginning to blacken and the mozzarella is brown and bubbly. Remove from the oven and allow the pizza to rest for 5 minutes. Add a generous pinch of flaky salt, scatter the oregano and basil over the whole pie, and serve.

BISTRO PORK

BISTRO PORK

It's funny that the designation "bistro" has survived four books—
really the recipes here aren't so much bistro as they are traditional Old World Europe. You'd be just as likely to find much of
this food in a Roman trattoria as you would in a Lyonnaise bistro.
Never mind that. This chapter is European comfort food, and the
word *bistro* encompasses this concept. You don't need any exotic
ingredients to cook these recipes—just plenty of shallots, French
vinegar, high-quality olive oil, the best butter you can afford,
and heavy cream that is not ultrapasteurized.

DRINKS

This chapter demands wine—French and Italian wine at that. (Okay,
you should have a pint with the pork pie and there are bargains
to be had in lighter reds made with old varietals coming out of
Spain and Portugal, which should not be overlooked.) Pork does best
with medium-bodied reds that are lower in tannin and alcohol. It
also works with more substantial whites, depending on the flavors
involved. For a chop with Madeira sauce, I'd go for a dry Riesling,
but the classic Italian pork braised in milk demands a worthy
Barolo. For the spaghetti with clams and belly, you really need
a Sauvignon Blanc with some backbone, a Chenin Blanc with clear
minerality, or a Pinot Noir worthy of the name. Whatever you do,
stick to the continent and don't forget that red need not be served
very warm, just as white should arrive at the table cool but not
icy (unless you're sweltering in the sun, quaffing a glass of
spritzy Vinho Verde, in which case an ice cube or two would not be
out of place).

ON THE TABLE

I won't repeat what I said about bread in my introduction to the
American chapter, but I could. Great bread and cold sweet butter
almost always belong on the table with the food in this chapter.
Ditto flaky salt, such as Maldon. Otherwise, my advice for enjoying
the food here is to indulge by making a long meal of it. Start
with a small first course—a composed salad with smoked fish and
greens or lots of cold roasted vegetables with toasted nuts—
and follow your meal with a nibble of redolent cheese. Sitting
at the table well into the night is an honorable, but too often
neglected, tradition.

SWEETS

I hardly need to prompt anyone reading this book to imagine the
endless possibilities for a terrific French or Italian dessert. Keep
it in country—make a semifreddo or elegant almond cake to go with
the Italian meal, and a tart, a light mousse, or some decadent chocolate gâteau to finish the French meals. If you can't be bothered,
at least buy some really intense chocolate—salted caramel is my
favorite. Break it into squares, and pass it around in a decorative
dish to nibble with the last remnants of wine.

MADEIRA-SAUCED RIB CHOPS,
FRENCH LENTILS, AND
HEADCHEESE-GHERKIN SALAD

SERVES 4

This is a hearty meal that's at once simple and elegant. The beauty
of it is that the ingredients do so much of the work for you—
between the Madeira, Puy lentils, and headcheese, you already have
a depth and range of flavors that need very little prodding to
coalesce into a coherent, tempting plate.

— MADEIRA-SAUCED RIB CHOPS —

FOUR 12-OZ TO 1-LB/340- TO 455-G BONE-IN RIB CHOPS, 1$^1/_2$ IN/4 CM THICK

1 TSP KOSHER SALT

1 TBSP ORGANIC HIGH-HEAT OIL (SEE HIGH-TEMPERATURE COOKING OILS, PAGE 17)

2 TBSP BUTTER

1 LARGE OR 2 SMALL SHALLOTS, CHOPPED

$^1/_2$ CUP/120 ML SERCIAL MADEIRA

$^1/_2$ CUP/120 ML MEAT OR POULTRY STOCK OR WATER

3 SPRIGS FRESH THYME

FLAKY SALT AND BLACK PEPPER FOR FINISHING

Preheat the oven to 300°F/150°C. Dry the chops, sprinkle them with
the kosher salt, and set them on the counter for 30 minutes to
1 hour to take the chill off. Heat a large cast-iron frying pan set
over high heat until very hot. Add the oil and, when it shimmers,
carefully place the chops in the pan. Cook for 4 to 6 minutes on
each side, or until the exterior is nicely browned. Set the chops in

$\Rightarrow$

the oven, pan and all, and finish cooking the meat gently for 12 to 15 minutes, or until an instant-read thermometer inserted into the thickest part of the chop reads 145°F/63°C. The meat is done when it's pink, but not bloody, and the texture is slightly granular, not slippery and smooth as it is when raw. Transfer the chops to individual plates and stick them in the oven with the heat off and the door open.

Without washing the pan, place it over medium heat and add the butter, shallots, Madeira, stock, and thyme. Cook to reduce the liquid by half, 5 to 7 minutes, scraping up any tasty brown bits from the bottom of the pan. Fish out the spent thyme sprigs, taste the sauce, and season with flaky salt and black pepper, as needed. Serve on warm plates, pouring the sauce over the chops.

— FRENCH LENTILS —

I've intentionally kept these lentils plain, because you're going to have so many flavors working together. These elegant legumes are the ideal medium for getting the most out of the pork, sauce, and salad.

2 TBSP BUTTER	1 CUP/200 G FRENCH PUY LENTILS
2 GARLIC CLOVES, THINLY SLICED	1/2 TSP KOSHER SALT
3 CUPS/720 ML CHICKEN STOCK OR WATER	

In a medium saucepan set over medium heat, combine the butter and garlic. Cook for 1 to 2 minutes, stirring. Do not brown. Add the stock and lentils, cover, and cook at a gentle simmer for 50 to 60 minutes, or until the lentils are tender. Stir in the salt and serve.

— HEADCHEESE-GHERKIN SALAD —

This salad is inspired by a memorably fine "elevenses" at the
St. John Bar and Restaurant, Trevor and Fergus Henderson's
venerable base in the old meat-market neighborhood of Smithfield,
in London. Buy the best headcheese you can find—a serious deli
is a good place to start unless, of course, you're making your
own. Put together a double batch of the versatile and pretty
Pickled Shallots, and throw them into scrambled eggs, a sandwich,
or virtually any salad.

PICKLED SHALLOTS

2 ELEPHANT SHALLOTS OR 4 REGULAR SHALLOTS,
CUT INTO VERY THIN ROUNDS

1 CUP/240 ML CIDER OR WHITE WINE VINEGAR

½ TSP SUGAR

1 TBSP MUSTARD SEED

1 TSP KOSHER SALT

1 LARGE BUNCH FRESH PARSLEY

12 GHERKINS, CUT INTO THIN ROUNDS

8 OZ/225 G HEADCHEESE, FINELY DICED

6 CHERRY BELLE RADISHES, GRATED (MOST ANY
VARIETY OF RADISH WILL DO)

2 TBSP BEST OLIVE OIL (SEE OLIVE OIL, PAGE 18)

1 TBSP GRAINY MUSTARD

BLACK PEPPER

To make the pickled shallots: Combine the shallots, vinegar, sugar,
mustard seed, and salt in a small bowl. Let sit for at least 1 hour
at room temperature, or up to 10 days in the refrigerator. Drain,
reserving 2 tbsp of the brine.

Tear the thick stems off the parsley and float the leaves, still
on their tender stems, in a large bowl of cold water. Swish them
around, changing the water once or twice to remove every trace of
grit, and then dry thoroughly. Pick the leaves off their stems and
place in a large mixing bowl. Add the gherkins, pickled shallots,
headcheese, and radishes.

In a small bowl, mix together the olive oil, reserved shallot brine,
and mustard. Pour the dressing over the salad, add plenty of black
pepper, and toss well. This is a salad that actually benefits from
sitting dressed for 30 minutes or so before serving.

BRINED RIB ROAST,
PORCINI BELUGA LENTILS, AND WATERCRESS SALAD

SERVES 4

This is the sort of plate I would serve when I have a special bottle of red wine stocked away for an elegant meal. There's something about the porcini, lentils, and fatty roasted meat that pushes this plate beyond the ordinary. I don't like to french a roast, since the delicious meat that's stripped away from those bones is wasted. I choose substance over looks when it comes to meat, dogs, and books—among other things.

— BRINED RIB ROAST —

ONE 4- TO 5-LB/1.8- TO 2.3-KG RIB ROAST (FRENCHED, IF YOU PREFER)

KOSHER SALT

4 TO 6 CUPS/1 TO 1.5 L COLD WATER

1 TSP ORGANIC HIGH-HEAT OIL (SEE HIGH-TEMPERATURE COOKING OILS, PAGE 17)

2 RIPE BARTLETT, BOSC, OR ANJOU PEARS

1 TBSP LEMON JUICE

1 SHALLOT, CHOPPED

1 CUP/240 ML BEEF, PORK, OR CHICKEN STOCK; WHITE WINE; OR WATER

THYME SPRIGS

FLAKY SALT AND BLACK PEPPER FOR FINISHING

Place the roast in a mixing bowl and cover with salt water using a ratio of 1 tbsp salt to 1 cup/240 ml water. Cover and refrigerate overnight (or, if you're short on time, brine the meat for as long as 2 hours on the counter). Allow the meat to rest at room temperature for 1 hour before removing it from the brine.

Preheat the oven to 400°F/200°C. Dry the meat thoroughly and rub all over with the oil. Place in a small roasting pan or cast-iron frying pan. Roast for 30 minutes, reduce the heat to 300°F/150°C,

and roast for another 35 to 45 minutes, or until the pork reaches an internal temperature of 140°F/60°C.

While the meat cooks, core and dice the pears, toss with the lemon juice, and reserve in a small bowl. When the roast is done transfer the meat to a plate and set it to rest in the oven with the oven door open and the heat off.

Place the roasting pan over medium-low heat without discarding the pan juices or rendered fat. Add the shallot to the pan and cook over low heat until just soft, 3 to 4 minutes. Scrape to loosen any tasty bits that may be stuck on the bottom of the pan as the shallot cooks. Add the stock, thyme sprigs, and pear along with any residual juices.

Reduce the sauce to about half of its original volume and remove from the heat. Carve the roast into thick slices, working the knife between the bones.

Place the meat on a warm platter, cover with the sauce, and season with flaky salt and black pepper. (I leave the thyme sprigs in the sauce, but if you don't like the rustic look remove them before bringing the platter to the table.) Serve immediately.

— PORCINI BELUGA LENTILS —

These petite black legumes evoke beluga caviar in appearance, but they are far more delicate in taste. The porcini add an earthy richness, making this is my latest favorite lentil combination.

½ CUP/10 G DRIED PORCINI MUSHROOMS

1½ CUPS/300 G BELUGA LENTILS

2 TBSP BUTTER

1 SHALLOT, CHOPPED

¾ TSP KOSHER SALT

Bring 2 cups/480 ml water to a boil and pour over the porcini in a small bowl. Set aside for 15 minutes. Put the lentils in a medium pot, cover with 2 cups/480 ml cold water, and bring to a boil over high heat. Turn off the heat and set to soak until the porcini are ready.

Transfer the porcini and their liquid to a blender and work for just a few seconds to pulverize. Add to the lentils, set them over medium-low heat, and simmer, uncovered, for 12 to 15 minutes, or until the lentils are tender but not mushy, and the water has evaporated. Watch carefully for scorching as the lentils finish cooking. Stir now and then, but not too much, as you'll break up the pretty lentils. Melt the butter in a small frying pan set over medium heat, add the shallot and salt, and sauté for 1 to 2 minutes, or until the butter begins to brown on the edges. Pour the hot butter over the lentils, stir gently, and serve.

— WATERCRESS SALAD —

You'll find two varieties of watercress sold commercially: the water-loving, branching stem variety, *Nasturtium officinale*; and field cress, *Lepidium campestre*, which has broad, spoon-shaped leaves. Both are peppery and delicious. Mix either one with radish—a close cousin botanically—and you'll have a gorgeous variation on the classic simplicity of a plain watercress salad.

1 BUNCH WATERCRESS, STEMMED (ABOUT 2 OZ/55 G OF LEAVES)

2 SMALL OR 1 LARGE CHERRY BELLE RADISH, COARSELY GRATED

2 TSP BEST OLIVE OIL (SEE OLIVE OIL, PAGE 18)

½ TSP CHAMPAGNE VINEGAR OR WHITE WINE VINEGAR

¼ TSP KOSHER SALT

Combine the watercress and radish in a mixing bowl and toss thoroughly with the olive oil, vinegar, and salt. Serve immediately.

MILK-BRAISED BONELESS LOIN ROAST
OVER POLENTA

SERVES 4

This is a taboo-busting combination of milk and pork, and yet it's a Northern Italian classic. Go figure. Don't skip the polenta if you want the whole gorgeous arrangement. Rich and creamy, this is a case for an Italian red wine—I'd go with a Chianti Classico or a Reserva if you're feeling flush.

— MILK-BRAISED BONELESS LOIN ROAST —

3 TBSP ORGANIC HIGH-HEAT OIL (SEE HIGH-TEMPERATURE COOKING OILS, PAGE 17)

2 TO 3 LB/910 G TO 1.4 KG BONELESS LOIN ROAST

KOSHER SALT

3 LARGE CARROTS, HALVED CROSSWISE AND THEN CUT INTO FINGER-SIZE BATONS

1 LARGE FENNEL BULB, CUT INTO $1/2$-IN/12-MM ROUNDS

1 HEAD GARLIC, CLOVES PEELED

3 SPRIGS FRESH THYME, PLUS 2 TBSP LEAVES

2 CUPS/480 ML WHOLE MILK

1 CUP/240 ML HEAVY CREAM

$1/4$ TSP RED PEPPER FLAKES

PINCH OF GROUND NUTMEG

BLACK PEPPER

POLENTA (RECIPE FOLLOWS) FOR SERVING

4 TBSP/60 ML TBSP BALSAMIC VINEGAR

FLAKY OR COARSE SALT FOR FINISHING

Preheat the oven to 250°F/120°C. Heat the oil in a large, deep (2 in/5 cm), ovenproof frying pan, cast-iron if you have it, set over medium heat. When it's hot, add the loin roast and cook for 3 to 4 minutes per side, or until the meat has browned all over. Don't be shy—it should be a light mahogany color for the best flavor. Drain off the fat (but don't wash the pan), salt the roast on all sides with kosher salt, and set it fatty-side up. Add the carrots, fennel, garlic, thyme sprigs, milk, cream, red pepper flakes, nutmeg, and plenty of black pepper to the pan. The meat should be half in and half out of the liquid.

Roast for 50 to 60 minutes, or until an instant-read thermometer inserted in the center reads 145°F/63°C. Transfer the meat and vegetables to a platter, discarding the spent thyme sprigs and reserving the liquid in the pan. Set the platter in the oven with the heat off and the door cracked. Place the pan over medium heat and simmer to reduce and caramelize the liquid, 8 to 12 minutes. You want to reduce the sauce without taking it too far—stop when it reaches a consistency you're happy with, even if it's not as dark as you'd like it. Watch carefully and once it begins to thicken, remove it from the heat. Taste and season with kosher salt and plenty of black pepper.

To serve, scoop some of the polenta in the center of each plate. Carve the meat, laying the slices over the polenta surrounded by carrots, fennel, and garlic cloves. Drizzle 1 tbsp of the balsamic over each portion of and then ladle the sauce over the meat. Scatter the thyme leaves over everything, and finish with a pinch of flaky salt. Pass the remaining sauce at the table.

— POLENTA —

This polenta should not aspire to distract from or interrupt the main attraction. With this in mind, I have aimed to make this polenta as buttery, rich, and delicious as a fresh croissant, but I have not made it with stock and I have not dolled it up with cheese.

1 CUP/140 G POLENTA	KOSHER SALT
8 CUPS/2 L WATER	2 TBSP BUTTER, PLUS MORE AS NEEDED

Combine the polenta, water, and 1 tsp salt in a saucepan set over medium heat. Use a whisk to stir now and again as the polenta begins to cook. After about 20 minutes, it will begin to make noisy, popping sounds as the bubbles burst on the surface. Depending on the kind of polenta you're cooking, it will need another 10 to 20 minutes, but be sure to watch carefully to prevent scorching. When it's cooked to a smooth consistency, without any hard bits of grain, add the butter and taste. Add more salt or butter, as you like. The polenta should be smooth, creamy, and fairly irresistible on its own. Turn off the heat and cover until ready to serve.

DRY-CURED-OLIVE-STUFFED TENDERLOIN
WITH CHICKPEA—BLACKENED PEPPER SALAD AND SPICY ROASTED HALLOUMI

SERVES 4

This Greek-inflected meal evokes an island somewhere in the Aegean, stripped bare by wild goats. Stranded there, I'd satisfy myself with this meal and a tall, cloudy glass of ouzo, diluted with frigid water. A bite of perfectly fresh, flaky baklava would complete my happiness when the meal is done.

— DRY-CURED-OLIVE-STUFFED TENDERLOIN —

ONE 1 1/2-LB/680-G TENDERLOIN

KOSHER SALT

4 TBSP/55 G BUTTER, AT ROOM TEMPERATURE

1/2 CUP/70 G DRY-CURED OLIVES, PITTED AND CHOPPED (MEASURE OR WEIGH BEFORE PITTING)

1 TSP CHOPPED FRESH ROSEMARY

2 ANCHOVY FILLETS, CHOPPED

2 GARLIC CLOVES, MINCED

ZEST OF 1 LEMON

1 TBSP ORGANIC HIGH-HEAT OIL (SEE HIGH-TEMPERATURE COOKING OILS, PAGE 17)

Dry the meat and cut it deeply down the center lengthwise, without cutting it into two pieces. Salt the meat inside and out and set aside on the counter. The meat should rest at room temperature for 30 minutes to take the chill off before going in the oven.

In a small bowl, mash together the butter, olives, rosemary, anchovies, garlic, and lemon zest. Distribute about two-thirds of the olive paste along the length of meat, taking care to separate the remaining third in a separate bowl so it doesn't come in contact with the raw meat. Pinch the two sides of the meat together, pressing the paste back into the meat. Cut a 5- to 6-ft/1.5- to 1.8-m length of butcher's string and tie a knot around one end of the meat, so that it holds the cut closed. Wrap the string around the meat four or five times to reach the other end. Switch back, making a crisscross pattern with the string. Tie the remaining end to the loose end of the initial knot.

Preheat the oven to 300°F/150°C. Heat the oil in a large ovenproof frying pan, preferably cast-iron, set over high heat. Place the meat, cut-side up, in the hot oil and cook until the bottom browns up nicely, 5 to 8 minutes. Transfer the meat, pan and all, to the oven. Roast for 15 to 20 minutes, or until the meat firms up slightly when poked. The internal temperature should be about 140°F/60°C, although it will be difficult to gauge because of the stuffing. Remove the meat from the oven and let it rest for 5 minutes before slicing. (It will gain several degrees as it rests on the counter.) Serve the slices with the reserved olive paste on the same plate.

— CHICKPEA-BLACKENED PEPPER SALAD —

Equal parts vegetable and bean, this is not just any bean salad.

1 1/2 LB/680 G SMALL SWEET PEPPERS, HALVED, SEEDED, AND CORED

3 TBSP VEGETABLE OIL

1 BUNCH BEET GREENS, CHOPPED

1/2 TSP RED PEPPER FLAKES

TWO 15-OZ/430-G CANS CHICKPEAS, RINSED AND DRAINED

3 TBSP BEST OLIVE OIL (SEE OLIVE OIL, PAGE 18)

3 TBSP RED OR WHITE WINE VINEGAR

1/2 CUP/20 G CHOPPED FRESH PARSLEY

2 TBSP FRESH OREGANO LEAVES

1/2 TSP KOSHER SALT

BLACK PEPPER

FLAKY SALT (OPTIONAL)

Preheat the oven to 500°F/260°C. Toss the peppers in a large mixing bowl with 1 tbsp of the vegetable oil. Spread out on a baking sheet and roast for 12 to 15 minutes, or until slightly blackened on the sides and bottom. (Don't let your fear of blackened food compel you to remove them from the oven before they're done!) Set aside to cool.

Set a large sauté pan over medium heat with the remaining 2 tbsp vegetable oil. When the oil is hot, add the greens and red pepper flakes and cook, stirring, for 2 to 3 minutes, or until the greens are just wilted. Transfer to a large mixing bowl and add the peppers along with the chickpeas, olive oil, vinegar, parsley, oregano, kosher salt, and a grind of black pepper. Mix thoroughly, taste and add a pinch of flaky salt (or a little more vinegar), as you wish, before serving.

— SPICY ROASTED HALLOUMI —

Strangely squeaky when you bite into it, this cheese is appealing for the marvel of grilling magic it demonstrates and for its briny sturdiness. The felicity of the salty cheese upon meeting chiles, lemon, mint, and black pepper is its most powerful attraction.

8 OZ/225 G HALLOUMI, SLICED 1/2 IN/12 MM THICK

2 TBSP ORGANIC REFINED OLIVE OIL
(SEE OLIVE OIL, PAGE 18)

1 TBSP RED PEPPER FLAKES

ZEST OF 1 LEMON

2 TSP FRESH LEMON JUICE

1/4 CUP/10 G FRESH CHOPPED MINT

BLACK PEPPER

Build a hot fire in a charcoal or wood grill or heat a gas grill to high. Use a clean, well-cured grate. In a small bowl, combine the halloumi, olive oil, and red pepper flakes. Be sure the cheese is coated on all sides.

Grill the cheese over the hot coals, heating each side for 2 to 4 minutes, or until the surface is marked and the cheese is lightly toasted. Place the grilled halloumi on a platter, and sprinkle with the lemon zest, lemon juice, mint, and plenty of black pepper. (Stay clear of salt—this cheese is quite salty.) Serve immediately.

FRESH HAM STEAKS
WITH RAW MUSHROOM SALAD AND
HAIGA RICE WITH SHALLOT BUTTER

SERVES 4

I much prefer my ham without smoke or sweet glaze. Here, the acidity of the Raw Mushroom Salad brightens the deliciously fatty meat. Fresh ham steaks are surprisingly difficult to come by. If you can't find them, bone the leg out of a fresh ham, separate the muscles—you can practically do this with your hands—and then slice the pieces to create the largest steaks possible. Seared on the stove top and finished slowly in the oven, this cut—usually cured and smoked—will surprise you with its charms.

— FRESH HAM STEAKS —

2 TO 3 LB/910 G TO 1.4 KG HAM STEAKS

1 TSP ORGANIC HIGH-HEAT OIL, PLUS 1 TBSP
(SEE HIGH-TEMPERATURE COOKING OILS, PAGE 17)

½ TSP KOSHER SALT

FLAKY SALT AND BLACK PEPPER FOR FINISHING

Preheat the oven to 300°F/150°C. (To grill, see the instructions for cooking Mayan Poc Chuc on page 145.) Dry the meat all over, coat with the 1 tsp oil and kosher salt, and rest on the counter for 30 minutes to 1 hour to take the chill off. Heat a cast-iron frying pan over high heat, add the remaining 1 tbsp oil and, when it shimmers, carefully place the steaks in the pan. Cook for 3 to 5 minutes on the first side, and 2 to 3 minutes on the second to brown the exterior. The meat may curl up on the edges; don't worry, just try to get a little color on it. Set in the oven, pan and all, for 5 to 7 minutes, or until the internal temperature

reaches 145°F/63°C. (Thick cuts, about 1½ in/4 cm, may take another 5 minutes or so.) The meat is done when it's pink, but not bloody, and the texture is slightly granular, not slippery and smooth as it is when raw. Finish with flaky salt and a grind of pepper. Serve immediately.

— RAW MUSHROOM SALAD —

I'm new to raw mushroom salad. Sure, I've eaten mushrooms that are essentially pickled on antipasti plates, but these mushrooms are truly animated—acidic, woody, and textured.

1 LB/455 G MIXED MUSHROOMS, SUCH AS PORTOBELLO, CREMINI, MAITAKE, AND SHIITAKE, SLICED VERY THIN

1 TSP KOSHER SALT

3 TBSP WHITE WINE VINEGAR

¼ CUP/60 ML ORGANIC REFINED OLIVE OIL (SEE OLIVE OIL, PAGE 18)

½ CUP/20 G FINELY CHOPPED FRESH PARSLEY

BLACK PEPPER

Put the mushrooms in a large mixing bowl. In a small bowl, whisk together the salt, vinegar, and olive oil. Pour the dressing over the mushrooms and toss to thoroughly coat. Let the mushrooms sit at room temperature for 10 minutes and toss again. They will begin to give up some of their moisture, which you'll see in the bottom of the bowl, along with the vinaigrette. Let the mushrooms sit for another 20 minutes, or refrigerate for up to 24 hours. Before serving, drain the mushrooms in a mesh strainer to get rid of the excess liquid (save it for a salad dressing!). Put the mushrooms in a serving bowl, toss with the parsley, and finish with a good grind of black pepper before serving.

— HAIGA RICE WITH SHALLOT BUTTER —

There are few foods that can compete, day after day, with buttery rice. Haiga rice is short-grain rice that's been milled with great care to preserve the protective germ. I like to think of it as the perfect compromise between white and brown rice.

1 CUP/190 G HAIGA RICE

3 TBSP BUTTER

1 LARGE SHALLOT, CHOPPED

1/2 TSP KOSHER SALT

FLAKY SALT AND BLACK PEPPER (OPTIONAL)

Rinse the rice in a small saucepan with a lid until the water is less cloudy. Drain, add 1 1/3 cups/315 ml water, cover, and set over medium-low heat for 12 to 15 minutes, or until the water has evaporated and the rice is tender. Melt the butter in a small frying pan set over low heat, add the shallot and kosher salt, and cook for 3 to 4 minutes, or until the shallot is soft. Don't brown the butter. Pour the shallot butter over the rice and fluff with a fork. Add a pinch of flaky salt and black pepper, if you wish, before serving.

GREMOLATA SHOULDER STEAKS,
CARAMELIZED FENNEL, AND SWEET PEPPERS

SERVES 4

Shoulder steaks are a down-market cut, which I like as a break from loin chops because they're fatty and flavorful. Too bad they're not so handsome. If you're planning a cozy family dinner, this is your cut. If you're cooking to impress, make the gremolata and put it on a thick, bone-in loin chop. Just be sure not to overcook your meat. A loin chop is much less forgiving than a shoulder steak.

— GREMOLATA SHOULDER STEAKS —

¼ CUP/60 G KOSHER SALT

1 TBSP SUGAR

4 CUPS/960 ML WATER

1½ TO 2 LB/680 TO 910 G SHOULDER STEAKS OR CHOPS (SUBSTITUTE RIB OR BONE-IN LOIN CHOPS)

2 GARLIC CLOVES, CHOPPED

FINELY GRATED ZEST OF 1 ORANGE

FINELY GRATED ZEST OF 1 LEMON

¼ CUP/10 G CHOPPED FRESH MINT

1 TBSP CHOPPED FRESH ROSEMARY

5 ANCHOVY FILLETS

2 LARGE OR 6 TINY CAPERS

1 TSP ORGANIC HIGH-HEAT OIL, PLUS 1 TBSP (SEE HIGH-TEMPERATURE COOKING OILS, PAGE 17)

COARSE OR FLAKY SALT AND BLACK PEPPER FOR FINISHING

In a flat baking dish or a mixing bowl, combine the kosher salt and sugar together with the water. Lay the meat in the liquid to brine for 2 hours on the counter or up to 24 hours in the refrigerator.

In a mortar, combine the garlic, orange zest, lemon zest, mint, rosemary, anchovies, and capers. Work the ingredients into a paste with the pestle, taking care to mash the garlic. (If you don't own a mortar and pestle, mince all the ingredients except the grated zests, transfer to a small dish, add the zests, and mash everything together with a fork.) Cover the gremolata and set aside.

Preheat the oven to 300°F/150°C. Blot any excess moisture from the meat and rub with the 1 tsp oil. Heat a large frying pan, preferably cast-iron, over high heat, add the remaining 1 tbsp oil and, when it shimmers, carefully place the steaks in the pan. Brown until they're the color of a walnut shell, 4 to 6 minutes for each side. To finish cooking, place them, pan and all, in the oven for 5 to 10 minutes, or until an instant-read thermometer inserted into the center of the thickest steak reads 140°F/60°C. The meat is done when it's pink, but not bloody, and the texture is slightly granular, not slippery and smooth as it is when raw. Let the meat rest for 5 minutes on the counter. (It will gain several degrees as it rests.)

Serve the steaks with a pinch of flaky salt, plenty of black pepper, and a generous coating of gremolata.

— CARAMELIZED FENNEL —

Raw or cooked, fennel is one of those foods that I'll take anytime, anywhere, in virtually any form. Even if the fennel in your produce aisle is a little sorry looking, by peeling away the outer layer you'll discover the reliably crispy reward awaiting your attention. You won't need the optional lemon zest if you're serving this fennel with the gremolata, but be sure to add it if that piquant sauce won't be on your plate.

3 OR 4 FENNEL BULBS, DEPENDING ON SIZE, TRIMMED AND VERY THINLY SLICED (USE A MANDOLINE IF YOU HAVE ONE), PLUS ¼ CUP/10 G LIGHTLY CHOPPED FRONDS

¼ CUP/60 G ORGANIC REFINED OLIVE OIL (SEE OLIVE OIL, PAGE 18)

1 TSP KOSHER SALT

FINELY GRATED ZEST OF 1 LEMON (OPTIONAL)

FLAKY SALT FOR FINISHING

In a large, heavy frying pan, ideally cast-iron, set over low heat, combine the fennel bulbs, olive oil, and kosher salt. Cook, stirring frequently, for 20 to 25 minutes, or until the fennel is a deep brown with some crispy, blackened edges. Transfer the fennel to a serving dish, add the lemon zest (if using), taste for salt, and add a pinch of flaky salt if needed. Finish by scattering a few fennel fronds over the top for color.

— SWEET PEPPERS —

These **potent, oily sweet peppers** are a welcome addition to salads, sandwiches, and meats of all kinds.

8 OZ/225 G SMALL SWEET PEPPERS, HALVED, SEEDED, AND CORED

1 TBSP ORGANIC HIGH-HEAT OIL (SEE PAGE 17)

1/2 TSP KOSHER SALT

1 GARLIC CLOVE, CRUSHED

1 TSP RED PEPPER FLAKES

2 TBSP CIDER VINEGAR

2 TBSP BEST OLIVE OIL (SEE OLIVE OIL, PAGE 18)

Preheat the oven to 500°F/260°C. Toss the peppers in a small mixing bowl with the high-heat oil and salt. Spread out the peppers on a baking sheet and roast for 12 to 15 minutes, or until slightly blackened on the sides and bottom. Transfer the peppers to a serving bowl and toss with the garlic, red pepper flakes, vinegar, and olive oil. These peppers are good served warm, at room temperature, or cold. You can store them, tightly covered and refrigerated, for 5 days or so.

WHITE BEAN, PORK SHOULDER, AND TOMATO STEW
WITH BIBB-AVOCADO SALAD

SERVES 4

There's plenty of beautiful, dark meat on the shoulder no matter what part of it you buy. Cooking tougher, fattier pork in simmering liquid is simple and nearly impossible to foul up. With so much aromatic fennel, thyme, and parsley—not to mention browned meat—your kitchen will be fragrant with hints of flavors to come. For a family dinner, I like the Bibb-Avocado Salad served alongside the stew on a separate plate. If you're up for a first course of salad or a cheese course after the meal with the salad served at the same time, by all means!

— WHITE BEAN, PORK SHOULDER, — AND TOMATO STEW

2 TBSP ORGANIC HIGH-HEAT OIL (SEE HIGH-TEMPERATURE COOKING OILS, PAGE 17)

3 TO 4 LB/1.4 TO 1.8 KG PORK SHOULDER, PARTIAL OR WHOLE, ANY PORTION, CUT INTO GENEROUS 1-IN/2.5-CM CUBES (TENDONS AND BIG CHUNKS OF FAT DISCARDED, AND BONES RESERVED; ABOUT 2 LB/905 G CUBED MEAT)

1 WHITE OR RED ONION, CHOPPED

1/2 HEAD GARLIC, CLOVES CRUSHED AND PEELED

6 CUPS/1.4 L PORK OR CHICKEN STOCK (SUBSTITUTE WATER IF YOU DON'T HAVE HOMEMADE STOCK)

1 1/2 CUPS/300 G DRIED WHITE BEANS (SUBSTITUTE CANNED BEANS)

2 LARGE TOMATOES, DICED

3 LARGE SPRIGS FRESH THYME

1/2 CUP/20 G CHOPPED FRESH PARSLEY

1 FENNEL BULB, TRIMMED AND CHOPPED

1 1/2 TSP KOSHER SALT

BLACK PEPPER

1 TBSP VERY GOOD WHITE WINE OR CHAMPAGNE VINEGAR

4 TBSP/55 G BUTTER, AT ROOM TEMPERATURE

4 SLICES LEVAIN, TOASTED

GRATED PARMESAN CHEESE FOR SERVING

2 TBSP CHOPPED FRESH OREGANO

Heat the oil in a large Dutch oven with a tight-fitting lid over high heat. Once it's hot, brown the meat until it has a crusty, walnut-brown exterior, working in batches so as not to crowd the pot. (If you cook too much meat at once, it will steam in its own liquid, not brown.) Transfer the cubes to a plate as they're done. Turn down the heat if you have too much smoke—you will have some smoke, for sure! (If your bones have been sliced and have a flat surface, brown them, too. If not, just add them to the pot with the stock.)

Reduce the heat to medium-low and add the onion to the hot pot. (Don't wash that pot!) Cook the onion for 10 to 12 minutes, or until soft and fragrant, stirring often with a rubber spatula to work at the brown coating on the bottom of the pot. Add the garlic and cook, stirring, for another 5 minutes. Return the meat to the pot, and add the stock, bones, white beans, tomatoes, and thyme sprigs. Bring the liquid to a boil and turn down the heat to a low simmer. Skim any scum that rises to the surface.

Cover the pot and simmer over medium-low heat for 1 hour and 15 minutes. Add the parsley, fennel, salt, and a generous grind of black pepper and cook, covered, for another 15 minutes. The fennel and the beans should be soft and the meat should be very tender. Remove the bones if you desire. Stir in the vinegar.

Butter the toast and lay a slice in the bottom of each bowl. Spoon the stew on top and serve with a sprinkling of Parmesan and a pinch of oregano.

— BIBB-AVOCADO SALAD —

The frequent appearance of avocado in this book is a reflection of my mild obsession with its rich flavor and unmatched creamy texture. For a double hit, splurge on a bottle of avocado oil, as I recently did. As a hiatus from the familiarity of olive oil, it's a welcome replacement in any salad. Here it underscores the flavor of the fruit itself, making the avocado shine more than ever.

1 HASS AVOCADO

1 TSP FRESH LEMON JUICE, PLUS 1 TBSP

1 LARGE HEAD BIBB LETTUCE, TRIMMED

1/2 TSP KOSHER SALT

1 TBSP AVOCADO OIL (OLIVE OIL IS FINE, TOO)

FLAKY SALT AND BLACK PEPPER

Slice the avocado into a small mixing bowl and toss with the 1 tsp lemon juice. Tear the lettuce into large pieces and place in a salad bowl. Toss with the remaining 1 tbsp lemon juice, the kosher salt, oil, and a grind of pepper. Scatter the avocado on top and serve sprinkled with a pinch of flaky salt.

BELLY, ROOT, AND SNAIL STEW
WITH MICROGREEN SALAD

SERVES 4

This Fergus Henderson-inspired winter stew transforms three simple ingredients into an elegant meal. The Ear Gear is rich, but when combined with the earthy sweetness of roasted root vegetables, the indescribable appeal of snails, and a hint of Madeira, it takes on a magnetism all its own.

— BELLY, ROOT, AND SNAIL STEW —

1 CELERY ROOT, PEELED AND DICED

2 PARSNIPS, PEELED AND DICED

1/2 BLACK OR RAINBOW RADISH, DICED

2 TBSP VEGETABLE OIL

KOSHER SALT

2 TBSP BUTTER OR LARD

2 LEEKS, WHITE AND TENDER GREEN PARTS ONLY, THOROUGHLY WASHED AND THINLY SLICED

ONE 7-OZ/200-G CAN FRENCH SNAILS (18 TO 24 SNAILS, OR ESCARGOTS), DRAINED

1/3 CUP/60 G FRENCH PUY LENTILS

1 RECIPE EAR GEAR (RECIPE FOLLOWS)

1 LB/455 G QUICK-COOKED BELLY (SEE PAGE 104)

1/4 CUP/60 ML MADEIRA, PREFERABLY SERCIAL

1 TSP WHITE WINE VINEGAR

BLACK PEPPER

Preheat the oven to 400°F/200°C. In a medium mixing bowl, toss together the celery root, parsnips, and radish with the vegetable oil and 1/2 tsp salt. Spread out the vegetables on a baking sheet and roast for 10 to 15 minutes, or until well browned on the edges. Set aside.

In the bottom of a Dutch oven, large saucepan, or small stockpot, heat the butter with the leeks over medium heat and cook until just soft. Add the roasted vegetables to the pot along with 1 tsp salt, the snails, lentils, and Ear Gear. (Don't leave behind the meaty bits—they're crucial.) Simmer, covered, over medium-low heat for 25 to 30 minutes, or until the lentils are tender. Stir in the pork belly, Madeira, vinegar, and a few grinds of black pepper and taste. The soup will almost certainly need additional salt. Serve hot.

EAR GEAR
4 CUPS/1 KG

4 LB/1.8 KG PORK PARTS, A MIX OF EARS, HOCKS, AND FEET

2 LB/910 G CHICKEN LEGS OR WINGS

1 HEAD CELERY

1 BUNCH FRESH PARSLEY

1 BUNCH FRESH THYME

1 TBSP BLACK PEPPERCORNS

1 ONION, QUARTERED

3 BAY LEAVES

5 CARROTS

ONE 3-IN/7.5-CM PIECE GINGER, PEELED

1/2 CUP/120 ML MADEIRA, PREFERABLY SERCIAL

Combine all the ingredients in a stockpot. Cover with water and set over medium heat. When the stock begins to give off some scum on its surface, turn the heat to low and begin skimming every 3 to 5 minutes, until no more scum appears. Now you can walk away and let the stock simmer for 3 to 4 hours. I usually cover the pot for the final hour or so, when the parts begin to stick up out of the liquid. Strain through a colander or sieve (a clear stock is not your goal), retaining both the liquid and the meat. Once the meat has cooled enough to handle, discard the vegetables and chicken parts and begin picking the edible meat off the pork bones. Combine the meat with the liquid and refrigerate until ready to use. It will keep, tightly sealed and refrigerated, for 1 week, or for 3 months frozen.

— MICROGREEN SALAD —

Sometimes in winter, when there aren't any local greens to be had, hydroponically grown microgreens are just the solution. Once you find a source, you'll discover a terrific variety, including radish, mustard, broccoli, basil, cucumber, mint, and various lettuce babies. They're so fragile you hardly want to dress them.

4 OZ/115 G MICROGREENS, ANY VARIETY

1 TBSP BEST OLIVE OIL (SEE OLIVE OIL, PAGE 18)

PINCH OF KOSHER SALT

Put the greens in a medium bowl and toss very gently with the olive oil and salt just before serving.

CLAM, BELLY, AND GARLIC SPAGHETTI
WITH MOZZARELLA IN CARROZZA AND ARUGULA SALAD

SERVES 4

Pork and clams are a revered combination, and rightly so. By adding loads of garlic and parsley and putting the whole over pasta, you'll have a lust-worthy plate. Here, you'll find the quick-cook method for pork belly, in case you don't have 4 to 5 hours to cook it at 200°F/95°C, as directed on page 67. This method works just fine and takes only half the time. The Mozzarella in Carrozza and Arugula Salad are the only sides you'll need, offering, respectively, rich, crispy deliciousness and a bright, peppery pop of flavor.

— CLAM, BELLY, AND — GARLIC SPAGHETTI

<u>QUICK-COOKED BELLY</u>

1 LB/455 G PORK BELLY

KOSHER SALT

12 CHERRYSTONE CLAMS,
OR 24 SMALLER CLAMS, RINSED
(DISCARD ANY THAT ARE EVEN SLIGHTLY OPEN)

2 CUPS/480 ML DRY WHITE WINE

1 CUP/240 ML WATER

1 LB/455 G SPAGHETTI OR ANGEL HAIR PASTA,
COOKED AL DENTE ACCORDING TO PACKAGE
DIRECTIONS AND DRAINED

OLIVE OIL FOR PASTA, PLUS 1/4 CUP/60 ML

KOSHER SALT

2 TBSP BUTTER

1/2 HEAD GARLIC, CLOVES CRUSHED, PEELED,
AND CHOPPED

1 SHALLOT, CHOPPED

1/2 CUP/20 G CHOPPED FRESH PARSLEY

1 TSP RED PEPPER FLAKES

BLACK PEPPER

To make the quick-cooked belly: Preheat the oven to 300°F/150°C. Put the belly and 1 tsp salt in a large saucepan and cover with cold water. Bring to a boil over high heat and skim any impurities that may rise to the surface. Cover, reduce the heat so that you have a low simmer, and cook for 1 hour. Remove the belly from the water and transfer to an ovenproof sauté pan or a baking sheet. Sprinkle on all sides with ½ tsp salt and roast for 1 hour, or until lightly browned and crispy on the outside. Cool for 5 to 10 minutes before slicing.

In a large pot with a lid, combine the clams, white wine, and water. Set over high heat, cover, and cook for 10 to 12 minutes (less for smaller clams), or until the clams have opened enough for you to get the meat out. Drain the clams and set them aside to cool, retaining the cooking liquid in a small bowl. When the clams are cool enough to handle, remove the meat, cut off the muscle on each side, and chop. (If the clams seem sandy, rinse them in the cooking water as you work.) When you're finished, set the chopped clams aside.

Return the cooking liquid to the pot, leaving behind any grit that may have settled to the bottom, and reduce for 15 to 20 minutes over high heat, or until reduced by about one-third. Transfer to a clear glass measuring cup or bowl, and set aside to allow any additional sand to settle.

Preheat the oven to 400°F/200°C. Slice the pork belly, and cut the slices into small dice. Place the pieces on a baking sheet or in an ovenproof sauté pan and bake for 5 to 7 minutes, or until crisp. Remove from the oven and sprinkle with a little salt—the pork should be irresistible all by itself.

Toss the drained noodles with plenty of olive oil, and season with a pinch of salt. Keep them warm.

In a large sauté pan set over medium heat, combine the butter, ¼ cup/60 ml olive oil, garlic, and shallot. Cook for 3 to 5 minutes, or until the garlic and shallot are just fragrant and softened, but not colored. Add the reduced cooking liquid from the clams, taking care to leave the sand and dirt behind. Add the parsley, red pepper flakes, and clams and bring to a simmer. Turn off the heat and portion out the pasta into shallow bowls. Spoon the sauce on top, giving each bowl a good bit of that flavorful liquid at the bottom of the pan. Place the diced pork on top, adding a generous grind of black pepper before serving.

— MOZZARELLA IN CARROZZA —

Gooey and irresistible, these little French toast-esque mozzarella sandwiches are a revelation. Use good, freshly made, salted mozzarella. No need to use mozzarella di bufala—but there's no harm in it, either. Feel free to omit the pepper flakes if you're feeding children or those with delicate palates.

2 TBSP BUTTER, AT ROOM TEMPERATURE

8 THIN SLICES WHITE BREAD

8 OZ/225 G MOZZARELLA, SLICED

1 TSP RED PEPPER FLAKES (OPTIONAL)

KOSHER SALT

1/2 CUP/65 G ALL-PURPOSE FLOUR

BLACK PEPPER

1/4 TSP CAYENNE PEPPER

1/2 CUP/120 ML WHOLE MILK

2 EGGS, LIGHTLY BEATEN

3 TBSP ORGANIC REFINED OLIVE OIL
(SEE OLIVE OIL, PAGE 18)

Butter the bread on one side, and then lay the mozzarella on the buttered side of 4 slices, tearing as needed to fit the square. Spread the red pepper flakes (if using) evenly over the mozzarella, and sprinkle with a pinch of salt. Top with the second slice of bread to make sandwiches, butter-side in. Lightly press the sandwiches together and cut off the crusts.

In a flat bowl, such as a pasta dish, mix the flour with 1/2 tsp salt, a grind of black pepper, and the cayenne. Pour the milk into a similar bowl and the eggs into another.

Heat the olive oil in a large sauté pan set over medium heat. Dip the sandwiches into the milk, one at a time, and then into the flour, and then the egg. Place them in the hot oil and cook for 3 minutes on each side, or until nicely browned all over. Cut into quarters and serve hot.

— ARUGULA SALAD —

As plain and complete as a glass of cold water, arugula needs no
fancy dressing or accompaniments when it's paired with such a
rich meal. Just toss your leaves with serious olive oil, a squeeze
of lemon, and a pinch of salt. You'll appreciate the peppery flavor
of the leaves virtually unadorned.

2 1/2 OZ/70 G BABY ARUGULA LEAVES

1 TBSP BEST OLIVE OIL (SEE OLIVE OIL, PAGE 18)

1/2 TSP FRESH LEMON JUICE (JUST A SQUEEZE)

1/4 TSP KOSHER SALT

Just before serving, toss together the arugula, olive oil, lemon
juice, and salt in a serving bowl. Pass the salad at the table or
serve on small side dishes.

BRAISED GIANT MEATBALLS OVER FARFALLINI
WITH GREEN GARLIC BAGUETTE

SERVES 4

This is a far cry from the traditional spaghetti and meatballs. Think instead of the richest, most tender veal and pork meatballs, cooked and served in a rich stock dotted with cherry tomatoes and poured over a thin layer of tiny bow-tie pasta, called farfallini. Using good quality tomatoes will show—in summer, the Sun Golds I grow are in everything I cook. In winter, grape or cherry tomatoes are often the best bet. This meal is worthy of an expensive Barolo, I swear.

— BRAISED GIANT MEATBALLS — OVER FARFALLINI

GIANT MEATBALLS

1 CUP/115 G SUPERFINE BREAD CRUMBS OR MATZOH MEAL

1 CUP/240 ML WHOLE MILK

1 CUP/220 G WHOLE SHEEP'S-MILK RICOTTA (FRESH, IF POSSIBLE; COW IS OK TOO)

1 EGG

1 TSP KOSHER SALT

1 TSP RED PEPPER FLAKES

BLACK PEPPER

1 SMALL SHALLOT, MINCED

2 OR 3 CLOVES GARLIC, MINCED

1/2 CUP/60 G PECORINO ROMANO

1/4 CUP/10 G CHOPPED FRESH PARSLEY

1 LB/455 G GROUND PORK

1 LB/455 G GROUND VEAL

1 RECIPE ENRICHED STOCK (PAGE 111)

8 OZ/225 G FARFALLINI (SUBSTITUTE ACINI DI PEPE, ORZO, OR SMALL SHELLS)

2 TBSP BEST OLIVE OIL (SEE OLIVE OIL, PAGE 18)

1/2 TSP KOSHER SALT

4 TO 6 FRESH BASIL LEAVES

GRATED PARMESAN CHEESE FOR TOPPING

FLAKY SALT AND BLACK PEPPER FOR FINISHING

To make the giant meatballs: In a large mixing bowl, combine the bread crumbs, milk, ricotta, egg, kosher salt, red pepper flakes, a generous grind of black pepper, the shallot, garlic, Romano cheese, and parsley. Mix well. Crumble the pork and veal together over the mixture and mix gently. You don't want to work the mixture vigorously or overwork it. Stop when it's just combined and is not completely uniform in color, showing, in places, some small contrast between the meat and cheese mixture.

Using your hands or an ice-cream scoop, form eight or nine rough tennis ball-size rounds, placing them gently on a parchment-lined or oil-coated baking sheet as you work. Each one will weigh between 5 and 6 oz/140 and 170 g. That said, don't fuss over the size! Cover and refrigerate if you won't be using them for another hour or more.

Heat the Enriched Stock in a sauté pan set over medium-low heat and gently tuck the meatballs into the hot liquid. They may be a little crowded, but as you place them, the liquid in the pot will rise and you'll be surprised how many fit. Cover the pot and cook for 10 to 12 minutes over low heat, with the liquid at an easy simmer. Use a slotted spoon to gently turn each meatball so that the tops that have been out of the liquid are submerged. Cover and cook for another 10 to 12 minutes, or until the meatballs are no longer pink in the center.

Cook the pasta according to the package directions, taking care to keep it al dente. Drain and toss the pasta with the best olive oil and kosher salt. Cover and set aside to keep warm until ready to serve.

Line each plate with a layer of farfallini, place a meatball or two on top, and then ladle over plenty of rich braising liquid. Roll the basil leaves into cigarette-like rounds and snip into threads, scattering some over each plate. Add a pinch of Parmesan, a pinch of flaky salt, and a final grind of black pepper and serve.

ENRICHED STOCK

2 ¼ CUPS/530 ML

3 TBSP ORGANIC REFINED OLIVE OIL
(SEE OLIVE OIL, PAGE 18)

1 LARGE SWEET ONION, SUCH AS A VIDALIA,
HALVED AND THINLY SLICED

2 CUPS/480 ML RICH STOCK (PAGE 181)

3 TO 6 GARLIC CLOVES, CRUSHED

1 TSP KOSHER SALT

1 1/2 LB/680 G CHERRY OR GRAPE TOMATOES

In a sauté pan set over medium-low heat, combine the refined olive
oil and onion. Cook, stirring frequently, for 12 to 15 minutes, or
until the onion is soft and beginning to stick together in a mass.
Transfer to a large Dutch oven (approximately 12 in/30.5 cm in
diameter). Add the Rich Stock, garlic to your taste, salt, and
cherry tomatoes. Cover tightly and simmer over low heat for
20 minutes. It will keep, refrigerated, for 3 days, or frozen
for up to 3 months.

— GREEN GARLIC BAGUETTE —

Garlic bread has all the virtues of great toast—which are many—
married with the tremendous appeal of garlic. I've made this one
bright green, which is a way of saying I've added a fresh, vegetal
undertone of parsley to balance all that good olive oil. I prefer
my garlic bread chewy and crisp, so I use a chewy, sour, French-
style bread—if you like yours soft, go Italian style.

1/2 CUP/30 G FRESH PARSLEY, MOSTLY LEAVES

8 GARLIC CLOVES, CRUSHED AND PEELED

1 GARLIC SCAPE (OPTIONAL)

1/2 CUP/120 ML ORGANIC REFINED OLIVE OIL
(SEE OLIVE OIL, PAGE 18)

1/2 TSP KOSHER SALT

1 LONG FRENCH BAGUETTE (16 TO 24 IN/
40.5 TO 61 CM), CUT IN HALF LENGTHWISE

Preheat the broiler on its lowest setting. Combine the parsley,
garlic, garlic scape (if using), olive oil, and salt in a blender
and work until smooth. Smear a thin layer on both halves of the
bread. Set the bread under the broiler, at least 6 in/15 cm from the
heat source, and cook until brown and crispy, 2 to 4 minutes. Watch
it carefully! Depending on the strength of your broiler, the bread
may be a charred disaster before you think to check it. Serve hot.

BABY PORK PIES
WITH ROASTED MUSTARD POTATOES AND APPLE-CELERY SALAD

SERVES 4

Pork pie is as British as Charles Dickens, but I can't bear to make a British-style pie. Oxymoron though it may be, I want a lighter pork pie. That means ricotta, rather than cheddar, three kinds of fresh herbs, fennel seed, and broccoli rabe. This pork pie is what I imagine Fellini would order on set if he wanted to please Dame Maggie Smith. It would make the mistake of being more Italian than British, but it would still be a pork pie and it might just be the best one she'd be lucky enough to eat. This pie lacks fealty to queen and country, but that's no reason to forego the venerable tradition of a "pie and a pint."

— BABY PORK PIES —

2 TBSP BUTTER

3 GARLIC CLOVES, CHOPPED

2 LEEKS, WHITE AND TENDER GREEN PARTS ONLY, THOROUGHLY WASHED AND FINELY CHOPPED

4 CUPS/190 G STEMMED AND CHOPPED BROCCOLI RABE

1/4 CUP/20 G DRIED APPLE, FINELY CHOPPED (USE A FOOD PROCESSOR IF THE APPLES ARE VERY DRY)

2 TSP RED PEPPER FLAKES

1 TSP CELERY SEED

1 TBSP FENNEL SEED

1 TSP KOSHER SALT

BLACK PEPPER

1/2 CUP/55 G SUPERFINE BREAD CRUMBS OR MATZOH MEAL

1 CUP/220 G *RICOTTA DEL PASTAIO* OR REGULAR RICOTTA (IF USING REGULAR, OMIT THE 1/4 CUP/60 ML MILK)

1/4 CUP/60 ML MILK

3 EGGS; 2 BEATEN TOGETHER, 1 BEATEN SEPARATELY

1 TBSP CHOPPED FRESH OREGANO

2 TBSP CHOPPED FRESH SAGE

2 TBSP FRESH THYME LEAVES

1 LB/455 G GROUND PORK

2 SHEETS PUFF PASTRY DOUGH, THAWED BUT STILL COLD

Melt the butter in a large sauté pan set over medium heat. Add the garlic, leeks, broccoli rabe, dried apple, red pepper flakes, celery seed, fennel seed, salt, and plenty of freshly ground black pepper. Cook, stirring frequently, until the mixture is soft and begins to stick to the pan, 8 to 10 minutes. Remove the pan from the heat and add the bread crumbs to the leek mixture.

Preheat the oven to 400°F/200°C. In a large mixing bowl, combine the ricotta, milk, the 2 beaten eggs, the oregano, sage, and thyme. Mix well. Add the leek mixture and the pork. Mix gently but thoroughly without overworking. (If you're working ahead, you should immediately refrigerate the filling at this point.) Fill four 1-cup/240-ml ramekins to *just* beneath the rim. Cut the puff pastry into four circles to fit the tops of the ramekins (or use a deep-dish 9-in/23-cm pie pan). You can use the bottom of an empty ramekin as a guide. Place the pastry round on top of the filling, tucking in the edges gently so they don't puff up and out. (No need for a vent.) Brush the crust with the remaining beaten egg and bake for 25 to 30 minutes, or until the top crust is golden brown and the center of a pie reaches 160°F/71°C on an instant-read thermometer. If you must, cut into the pie to be sure the center is done. You're looking for a firm filling with no pink juices. Allow the pies to cool for 5 minutes before serving.

— ROASTED MUSTARD POTATOES —

So long as you have fresh, firm potatoes and plenty of high-quality olive oil, you can't go wrong roasting potatoes at a high temperature. I like this version because it has a little acidity, which brings the richness of potatoes to life.

2 TBSP MUSTARD, PREFERABLY BROWN

1 TBSP BALSAMIC VINEGAR

3 TBSP ORGANIC REFINED OLIVE OIL
(SEE OLIVE OIL, PAGE 18)

1 TSP KOSHER SALT

1 1/2 LB/680 G SMALL NEW POTATOES

FLAKY SALT AND BLACK PEPPER FOR FINISHING

Preheat the oven to 400°F/200°C. In the bottom of a large mixing bowl, whisk together the mustard, vinegar, olive oil, and kosher salt. Add the potatoes and toss until coated. Dump the potatoes onto a baking sheet, setting aside the bowl without washing. Roast the potatoes for 30 to 40 minutes, depending on their size. Insert a paring knife

into the center of the largest tuber to test for doneness—it's done
if the knife slides right in, without any resistance. Return the
potatoes to the mixing bowl to pick up the remaining mustard
vinaigrette, toss with flaky salt and a few grinds of black pepper,
and serve.

— APPLE-CELERY SALAD —

I can't decide whether this salad is better when made with apples
or pears. You can decide for yourself or mix the two and have all
the advantages of each one. I call for apples here only because
everyone has access to good apples, while getting a perfectly
ripe pear to the table takes skill, time, luck, and patience
(not necessarily in that order!).

1 LARGE BUNCH PARSLEY

1 GRANNY SMITH OR OTHER TART APPLE, PEELED,
CORED, AND DICED (OR 1 OR 2 ANJOU PEARS)

1 TBSP FRESH LEMON JUICE

1 HEAD CELERY, TOUGH OUTER STALKS REMOVED

¼ TSP KOSHER SALT

BLACK PEPPER

2 TBSP BEST OLIVE OIL (SEE OLIVE OIL, PAGE 18)

Float the parsley in a large mixing bowl filled with cold water
to remove any remaining grit. Dry the parsley and meticulously
pick the leaves off the stems. In a medium mixing bowl, combine the
apple with the lemon juice and toss to coat. Remove the bottom of
the celery and then, holding the whole bunch tight, cut into thin
slices, stopping when you reach the tough ends. The leaves are an
excellent addition. Add the celery and parsley to the bowl with
the apple and toss with the salt, a grind of black pepper, and the
olive oil. It's ready to eat.

LATIN PORK

LATIN PORK

Like the Bistro and American chapters, this one encompasses a ridiculously wide range of cuisines, from Cuban to Brazilian. Nonetheless, there is a shred of logic to it. As you'll find when you cook or read your way through this section, the recipes cling together through a set of shared ingredients: black beans, chiles, cilantro, coriander seed, cumin, and corn. I adore this kind of rich, bold, frequently spicy food. Fresh ingredients and a little attention to detail will make your home-cooked tacos, burritos, and stews surpass most any you've eaten out—unless, I suppose, you're a big traveler and have eaten well at the source. Have plenty of dried chiles (pasilla, Anaheim, ancho), fresh chiles (serrano, jalapeño, habañero), canned chipotles, queso fresco, and fresh cilantro at the ready. And for the feijoada, you'll need *farofa* (manioc flour), *azeite de dendê* (palm oil), and some tricky-to-locate Brazilian hot sauces, such as *malagueta* and *pimenta mista*; the best source is Amigofoods.com.

DRINKS

Beer, booze, and plenty of limes are the first order of business. Pour a beer over ice, add a drop of hot sauce, the juice of a lime, and you have a *michelada* (rim the glass with salt if you're really thirsty). This is a hard-to-beat drink in the heat of summer or midmeal after consuming one too many chiles. If you make mixed drinks, such as the Caipirinha (page 153) or a classic margarita, keep the citrus fresh and reach for high-quality booze. You'll reap the rewards as you drink, and the morning after no less.

ON THE TABLE

Wrap your tortillas in foil and let them warm slowly in the oven. They should almost invariably be on the table as a means of wrapping meat and sopping up sauce. In addition, keep a range of hot sauces and bowls of sliced jalapeños or serranos with a squeeze of lime juice, lime wedges, extra chopped cilantro, and crema available at all times. Even better, make a batch of your own hot sauce by combining chiles, lime juice, and a pinch of salt in a jar. This homemade version is flavorful, bright, and as hot as you want it to be. Keep it the refrigerator for a week—it starts to lose its heat

ST. LOUIS RIBS WITH ADOBO,
MIAMI TURTLE BEANS, AND BLACK RICE WITH MINT, CAULIFLOWER, AND BELL PEPPER

SERVES 4

In winter, making ribs in the oven makes me more than happy. Maybe it's because mastering the miracle of crispy, fatty pork on the bone without much trouble feels so good. If you've never made oven ribs, try it just once. I think you'll hardly miss the tasty flavor of hardwood smoke so long as you have a good, spicy sauce.

— ST. LOUIS RIBS WITH ADOBO —

4 TO 5 LB/1.8 TO 2.3 KG ST. LOUIS-CUT RIBS OR SPARERIBS (2 OR 3 SLABS), SILVERSKIN REMOVED (SEE THE INSTRUCTIONS ON PAGE 15)

KOSHER SALT

3 DRIED CHILES, SUCH AS ANCHO, PASILLA, OR GUAJILLO, STEMMED AND SEEDED (OR NOT, DEPENDING ON HOW SPICY YOU WANT YOUR SAUCE)

3 PLUM TOMATOES, CANNED OR FRESH

1 TSP SUGAR

3 TO 6 GARLIC CLOVES, DEPENDING ON SIZE

2 TBSP ORGANIC HIGH-HEAT OIL (SEE PAGE 17)

2 TSP DRIED OREGANO, PREFERABLY MEXICAN

BLACK PEPPER

Preheat the oven to 200°F/95°C. (If you prefer to grill, see the instructions on page 39). Place the ribs on a baking sheet, meaty-side up, sprinkle both sides with salt, and set aside for 30 minutes to

1 hour to take the chill off. Heat a small cast-iron pan over high heat until it's very hot. Put the chiles in the pan, toasting them on both sides until fragrant, without burning them all over—a little black is okay. Combine the chiles, 1/2 tsp salt, the tomatoes, sugar, garlic, oil, oregano, and a generous amount of black pepper in a blender or the bowl of a food processor. Work until smooth, 30 seconds to 1 minute. Use half the sauce to coat the ribs on both sides, and reserve the rest.

Bake the ribs for 3 to 3½ hours, turning them over halfway through. They should be falling-off-the-bone tender and crispy on the outside. (Smaller or thinner ribs may take less time.) When the ribs are done, give them a light coating with some of the reserved sauce and bake for another 5 minutes, just to heat the sauce. Cut the ribs into three-rib sections or leave the slabs whole, as you like. Transfer to a platter and serve, passing the extra sauce.

— MIAMI TURTLE BEANS —

There's nothing restrained about the wild, colorful culture of Miami, just as there's nothing restrained about these beans. With cheese on top and stirred in during cooking, they hit your palate as creamy, substantial, and immoderate.

2 TBSP LARD OR VEGETABLE OIL	7 TO 8 CUPS/1.7 TO 2 L WATER
1 RED OR YELLOW ONION, COARSELY CHOPPED	KOSHER SALT
3 LARGE GARLIC CLOVES, CRUSHED	6 OZ/170 G COTIJA CHEESE
2½ CUPS/455 G DRIED BLACK TURTLE BEANS	

In a medium frying pan set over medium heat, combine the lard and onion. Sauté, stirring frequently, until the onion is soft and lightly browned, 10 to 12 minutes. Transfer the onion to a large saucepan with a lid and add the garlic, beans, and 7 cups/1.7 L of the water. Bring to a boil, skimming any scum that rises to the top. Reduce the heat, cover, and simmer until the beans are tender, stirring occasionally and checking to be sure the beans are not drying out, 50 to 60 minutes. Add additional water, 1/2 cup/120 ml at a time, if the beans stick or dry out before they are done.

Transfer half the beans to a blender or food processor and work until smooth, 1 to 2 minutes. Work in two batches if you need to. Use caution when blending the hot beans. Return the blended beans to the pot and stir in 1½ tsp salt. Cut or crumble 4 oz/115 g of the cheese into chunks about the size of large jelly beans. Stir into the beans until the cheese melts. Don't overmix it, since the blobs of cheese are delicious. Taste for salt, adding a little more as needed. Serve with the remaining cheese finely grated on top.

— BLACK RICE WITH MINT, CAULIFLOWER, — AND BELL PEPPER

Every day there seems to be yet another trendy grain that's supposed to be healthful and tasty. I don't always find these grains tasty, however healthful they may be, but black rice is the exception. It's a grain well worth eating and it's pretty to boot.

1 1/2 CUPS/310 G BLACK RICE, RINSED AND DRAINED

3 CUPS/720 ML WATER

KOSHER SALT

1/2 CUP/120 ML ORGANIC REFINED OLIVE OIL (SEE OLIVE OIL, PAGE 18)

2 TBSP CIDER OR WHITE WINE VINEGAR

1 TBSP RED PEPPER FLAKES

3/4 CUP/30 G CHOPPED FRESH MINT

4 GARLIC CLOVES, CRUSHED AND PEELED

1 MEDIUM HEAD CAULIFLOWER, STEMMED AND BROKEN INTO SMALL, BITE-SIZE FLORETS

1 ORANGE BELL PEPPER, CORED AND SLICED INTO THIN ROUNDS

1/2 LEMON

Preheat the oven to 450°F/230°C. In a medium saucepan with a tight-fitting lid, combine the rice, water, and 1/2 tsp salt. Cover and set over medium heat. Cook for 30 to 35 minutes, or until the water has evaporated and the rice is tender but still chewy.

While the rice cooks, combine 1/2 tsp salt, the olive oil, vinegar, red pepper flakes, 1/2 cup/20 g of the mint, and the garlic in a blender and work until smooth. Put the cauliflower in a large mixing bowl and toss with roughly two-thirds of the dressing to coat. Spread out on a baking sheet (lined with parchment if you like). Using the same bowl, toss the bell pepper with the remaining dressing and lay on a separate baking sheet. Put both baking sheets of vegetables in the oven. Roast the cauliflower until it shows very dark spots on the edges, 8 to 12 minutes. Roast the bell pepper until it's just soft, but not dark, about 8 minutes.

Transfer the rice to a large serving bowl and toss with the cauliflower and bell pepper. Squeeze the lemon for juice and taste for salt, adding a pinch if needed. Finish by sprinkling with the remaining 1/4 cup/10 g chopped mint before serving.

GRILLED BONE-IN CHIPOTLE RIB CHOPS
WITH SPICY TOMATILLO SALSA AND SALTY-SWEET PLANTAINS

SERVES 4

If you cook your chops over indirect heat, slow and easy, the way you'd cook meat from the shoulder, a fresh ham, or ribs, you'll be very pleased with yourself—and your results. Cook your Salty-Sweet Plantains at the same time, while the fire is at its best. This brine will burn over direct heat—beware! Versatile, it will also take to any slow-cooked meat that wants to be a little spicy, sweet, and smoky. If you like, add a starch to this meal. Warmed corn tortillas would be welcome, as would Yellow Rice (page 137) and Miami Turtle Beans (page 122).

— GRILLED BONE-IN CHIPOTLE RIB CHOPS —

FOUR 12- TO 14-OZ/ 340- TO 400-G BONE-IN RIB CHOPS, 1 TO 1½ IN/2.5 TO 4 CM THICK

1½ TSP KOSHER SALT

¼ CUP/60 ML CIDER VINEGAR

2 CHIPOTLE CHILES IN ADOBO SAUCE, DRAINED, PLUS 2 TBSP ADOBO SAUCE

1 TBSP BROWN SUGAR (DARK OR LIGHT)

1 TBSP HOT SAUCE

3 GARLIC CLOVES

1 BUNCH FRESH CILANTRO STEMS

1 TBSP ORGANIC HIGH-HEAT OIL (SEE HIGH-TEMPERATURE COOKING OILS, PAGE 17)

Dry the chops, use 1 tsp of the salt to season them, and set them out on the counter for 30 minutes to 1 hour to take the chill off.

In a blender or food processor, combine the vinegar, chiles and adobo sauce, brown sugar, hot sauce, the remaining 1/2 tsp salt, the garlic, cilantro stems, and oil. Blend until smooth. Pour the sauce over the chops, turning to coat them all over. Allow the meat to rest on the counter for up to 1 hour, or marinate in the refrigerator for up to 24 hours. (Be sure to take the chops out of the refrigerator 30 minutes to 1 hour before cooking if you marinate it in the refrigerator.)

Build a medium fire in a charcoal or wood grill or heat a gas grill to medium. If you're using charcoal or wood, you want hot embers, not flames. (If you don't have a grill large enough to place the meat away from the heat source, make a small fire or set the gas grill to its lowest setting.) Use a clean, well-cured grate.

Place the chops over indirect heat. Cover the grill, and try to maintain the temperature in the grill so it hovers between 250 and 300°F/120 and 150°C. Cook the chops for 15 to 20 minutes on the first side, and turn and cook for an additional 10 to 15 minutes on the second. Cooking times will vary greatly, depending on the intensity of the fire, the thickness of the chops, and their temperature when they go on the grill. If the chops lack a nice crust or char, set them over direct heat for 3 to 5 minutes a side. Test for doneness by cutting into a chop, or use an instant-read thermometer if the meat is cut thick enough. Aim for 145°F/63°C. The chops should be a little pink in the center and juicy.

Remove the chops from the grill and let them rest for 5 minutes before serving.

— SPICY TOMATILLO SALSA —

This sauce makes up for its drab looks with its subtle lemon-pear-tomato essence. With notes of cumin and plenty of heat, it's phenomenal on pork.

1 LB/455 G TOMATILLOS, HUSKS REMOVED

1 TBSP ORGANIC HIGH-HEAT OIL (SEE HIGH-TEMPERATURE COOKING OILS, PAGE 17)

1/2 TSP KOSHER SALT

1 OR 2 DRIED CHILES, STEMMED AND SOAKED IN BOILING WATER FOR 5 TO 10 MINUTES, DRAINED, AND CHOPPED

1 TBSP CUMIN SEED, TOASTED

JUICE OF 1/2 LIME

Preheat the oven to 500°F/260°C. Toss the tomatillos in a medium mixing bowl with the oil and salt. Spread out the fruit (yes, it's a fruit) on a baking sheet (lined with parchment if you like) and roast for 20 to 25 minutes, or until the tomatillos have collapsed and are beginning to blacken in spots. Set aside to cool for a minute or two before removing the tough stems. Leave the liquid behind on the baking sheet and transfer the tomatillos to a blender. Add the chiles, cumin seed, and lime juice. Blend briefly—just enough to turn the chiles and tomatillos into a coarse sauce. Refrigerate for up to 2 days if not using right away.

— SALTY-SWEET PLANTAINS —

I don't use plantains much, but when I do, I'm never sorry to have their sweet, starchy presence on my plate to round out the other flavors.

2 RIPE PLANTAINS RIPENED TO A RICH YELLOW AND BLACK, PEELED

2 TBSP BUTTER, MELTED

FLAKY SALT

Rub the plantains all over with a little of the butter and set over a medium fire. You want them to brown, even blacken in spots, but also to cook slowly so that the fruit doesn't burn before it softens at the center. Turn and paint with butter as often as possible. Depending on the intensity of your fire, the plantains may take as little as 15 minutes or as long as 25 minutes to cook. Slice on the diagonal and serve hot, with a good pinch of salt.

POSOLE
WITH GREEN ONION QUESADILLAS

SERVES 4

To my palate, posole is defined by its acidity. Agreed, the hominy
is pretty great, as are the chunks of pork. But in the end the
acidity crossing the spice is what makes this soup worth cooking
and eating as often as you crave it—which is not infrequently
in my case. Give some major love to your stock and the rest
will fall into place.

— POSOLE —

2 DRIED ANCHO OR GUAJILLO CHILES, STEMMED AND SEEDED (OR NOT, IF YOU WANT IT SPICY)

KOSHER SALT

1 LB/455 G RIB CHOPS, SHOULDER (SUCH AS PORK BUTT), OR FRESH HAM, CUT INTO BITE-SIZE PIECES

2 TO 3 TBSP ORGANIC HIGH-HEAT OIL (SEE HIGH-TEMPERATURE COOKING OILS, PAGE 17)

1/2 HEAD GARLIC, CLOVES CRUSHED, PEELED, AND THINLY SLICED

1 RED OR ORANGE BELL PEPPER, DICED

6 CUPS/1.4 L PORK OR CHICKEN STOCK

3 CUPS/510 G CORN KERNELS, FRESH OR FROZEN

1 1/2 CUPS/425 G WHITE OR YELLOW HOMINY, RINSED

12 CHERRY TOMATOES, RED OR ORANGE, HALVED

JUICE OF 2 LIMES

3 OZ/85 G TORTILLA CHIPS, LIGHTLY CRUSHED

1 HASS AVOCADO, PITTED AND THINLY SLICED

1/4 CUP/10 G CHOPPED FRESH CILANTRO

6 GREEN ONIONS, TRIMMED TOP AND BOTTOM AND THINLY SLICED (USE IT ALL)

6 OZ/170 G COTIJA CHEESE, GRATED

Place a cast-iron pan over high heat. When the pan is hot, add the
chiles and toast until fragrant, without burning them, 3 to 5 minutes. Turn off the heat and cover the chiles with water. Set aside
to soak for at least 20 minutes.

Use about 1/2 tsp salt to season the meat. Place a sauté pan with 2 tbsp
oil in it over high heat. When the oil shimmers, add the meat and
cook until nicely browned. Work in batches if necessary so as not
to crowd the meat. Transfer to a plate and set aside. Use the same

pan, set over low heat, to briefly sauté the garlic for 1 to 2 minutes, or until just fragrant. Transfer to the plate with the meat (put it right on top if you like). Turn up the heat under the pan, add a little more oil, and sauté the bell pepper until it shows a little color on the edges.

Pulverize the chiles and the water in which they were soaking, using either a blender or a food processor. Pour the liquid into a large saucepan or stockpot set over medium heat. Add the stock, 1 tsp salt, the corn, hominy, and cherry tomatoes, along with the pork, garlic, and bell pepper. Cover and simmer gently for 30 to 40 minutes, or until the meat is very tender.

Add the lime juice and taste the soup for salt, adding a pinch if necessary. Ready four large soup or pasta bowls. Line each bowl with tortilla chips, using just half, while reserving the remainder to sprinkle on top. Ladle the soup into the bowls. Lay several slices of avocado across the top of each portion, and sprinkle with the remaining chips, the cilantro, green onions, and cheese. You could also serve the soup without toppings and bring them all to the table to pass, letting people doctor their own soup as they like.

— GREEN ONION QUESADILLAS —

The childish pleasures of quesadillas are many. For a tease of rich, round, cheesy gratification to go with the posole, I can't think of anything better. Add a few thinly sliced serranos or jalapeños if you want to make yours a little more grown-up.

4 FLOUR TORTILLAS, 8 IN/20 CM IN DIAMETER

8 OZ/225 G QUESO QUESADILLA, THINLY SLICED (SUBSTITUTE CHEDDAR)

12 GREEN ONIONS, TRIMMED TOP AND BOTTOM AND THINLY SLICED (USE IT ALL)

Set a cast-iron griddle or frying pan over medium heat. Once the griddle is hot, lay a tortilla down and lay half the cheese over it, covering the surface entirely. Sprinkle on half the green onions and then lay another tortilla on top. Cook for 3 to 6 minutes a side, or until the tortilla is crispy and browned. Allow the quesadilla to cool for a minute or two before cutting into eight pieces. Repeat with the remaining tortillas, cheese, and green onions. Serve immediately.

PORK MOLE NEGRO
WITH CHEESE AREPAS

SERVES 4

Mole seems difficult because there are so many ingredients to brown, toast, or blacken. Okay, but think of making mole as a series of basic steps: browning, toasting, blending, and slow cooking. Simple. I've done my best to make this recipe as rational as possible without cheating. That means toasting various ingredients at the same time, or blackening them, and not fussing like an unsupervised child over insignificant details. Surprisingly, given the presence of three chiles, with their seeds, this mole is not all that spicy. If you want more heat, throw a fresh serrano or jalapeño in the blender. The Cheese Arepas and Yellow or Green Rice, along with the condiments, make a decadent fiesta worthy of your labor.

— PORK MOLE NEGRO —

3 LB/1.4 KG PORK SHOULDER, FRESH HAM, OR RIB-END LOIN MEAT, CUBED

1½ TSP KOSHER SALT

ABOUT 4 TBSP/60 ML ORGANIC HIGH-HEAT OIL (SEE HIGH-TEMPERATURE COOKING OILS, PAGE 17)

2 DRIED GUAJILLO CHILES, STEMMED

1 DRIED ANCHO CHILE, STEMMED

3 CUPS/720 ML VERY HOT OR BOILING WATER

1 TOMATO, THICKLY SLICED

1 ONION, THICKLY SLICED

⅓ CUP/45 G ROASTED SALTED PEANUTS

2 TBSP SESAME SEEDS

¼ CUP/25 G SLICED ALMONDS (WHOLE ARE FINE)

½ PLANTAIN RIPENED TO A DEEP YELLOW

1 CORN TORTILLA, 6 IN/15 CM IN DIAMETER

1 SERRANO CHILE, STEMMED (OPTIONAL)

STEMS OF 1 BUNCH FRESH CILANTRO

¼ CUP/35 G RAISINS

1 TSP DRIED OREGANO (MEXICAN IF POSSIBLE)

¼ TSP GROUND CINNAMON

½ OZ/15 G UNSWEETENED CHOCOLATE

FOR THE TABLE

YELLOW RICE (PAGE 137) OR GREEN RICE (PAGE 142)

6 GREEN ONIONS, THINLY SLICED (USE IT ALL)

2 SERRANO CHILES, THINLY SLICED

½ CUP/20 G CHOPPED FRESH CILANTRO

1 CUP/240 ML CREMA

6 RADISHES, SOAKED IN ICE WATER FOR 10 TO 15 MINUTES AND SLICED

12 TO 16 CORN TORTILLAS, 6 IN/15 CM IN DIAMETER, WRAPPED TIGHTLY IN FOIL AND HEATED IN 200°F/95°C OVEN

Season the meat all over with ½ tsp of the salt. Heat a large cast-iron pan over high heat. When the pan is hot, add 1 tbsp of the oil and just enough meat to fit in the pan with plenty of space between the pieces. Brown the meat in three or four batches, 4 to 6 minutes for each batch. Add additional oil as needed. As you work, transfer the browned meat to a plate.

Once the meat is browned, add the guajillo and ancho chiles to the pan and heat until fragrant and beginning to color. Transfer the chiles to a bowl and cover with the hot water.

In the same pan, blacken the tomato and onion on both sides over high heat, 8 to 10 minutes. (Do not add any additional oil. The kitchen may be quite smoky at this point—no matter.) Transfer the tomato and onion to a large mixing bowl. Put the peanuts, sesame seeds, and almonds in the hot pan, shaking or stirring frequently until toasted, 1 to 2 minutes. Transfer to the mixing bowl with the tomato and onion. Halve the plantain lengthwise. Lay the halved plantain, the tortilla, and serrano (if using) in the hot pan, and toast them until blackened in spots. Transfer to the mixing bowl with the other blackened ingredients. Add the cilantro stems, raisins, and oregano.

Drain the guajillo and ancho chiles, reserving the water. Working in two or three batches, blend the reserved chile water and guajillo and ancho chiles with the blackened ingredients in the mixing bowl. Use the chile water sparingly, reserving enough for each batch to blend easily until very smooth, about 1 minute per batch. Transfer the blended sauce to a large saucepan, and add the meat, cinnamon, chocolate, and the remaining 1 tsp salt. Stir thoroughly and set over very low heat. You want the mole to simmer gently—use a heat diffuser if you need to. Cook, uncovered, for about 1 hour and 30 minutes (or a little less), stirring occasionally and scraping the bottom to be sure it's not scorching. When the sauce begins to bubble and pop like porridge, spattering all over your stove, it's ready. The meat should be tender and the sauce, intense. Serve with or over Yellow or Green Rice and put the green onions, sliced serranos, chopped cilantro, crema, radishes, and tortillas on the table to pass when serving.

— CHEESE AREPAS —

This is my basic recipe for what are essentially hot cornmeal pancake sandwiches with cheese. I encourage you to mix these up a little by adding sliced serranos, toasted cumin seed, green onions, or any exotic extra you can think of. These cakes are brought to life with a dollop of Cilantro-Tequila Crema (page 143), which also refreshes the mole.

2 EGGS	1 TSP SUGAR
2 1/2 CUPS/600 ML MILK	1/2 TSP BAKING POWDER
2 TBSP BUTTER, MELTED	1/2 TSP KOSHER SALT
2 CUPS/280 G FINELY GROUND CORNMEAL	1/4 TSP CAYENNE PEPPER
1/2 CUP/60 G FLOUR	7 OZ/200 G MOZZARELLA, SLICED (USE QUESO QUESADILLA IF YOU PREFER)
1/2 CUP/50 G GRATED COTIJA CHEESE	

Preheat the oven to 250°F/120°C. In a medium mixing bowl, beat together the eggs, milk, and butter. Add at once, without stirring, the cornmeal, flour, grated cheese, sugar, baking powder, salt, and cayenne. Stir everything together thoroughly without over-working the batter, and let it rest for 5 or 10 minutes before making the pancakes.

Heat a cast-iron griddle over medium heat until hot. Cover the sur-face of a baking sheet with aluminum foil and set aside. Place a little dollop of batter on the griddle to test the heat. If it browns up nicely in a minute or less, your griddle is ready. Working in batches, form pancakes with roughly the circumference of a tennis ball. Cook for 1 or 2 minutes, until the bubbles appearing on the surface are beginning to set. Flip and cook the other side until golden brown, 30 seconds to 1 minute. Transfer the cooked pancakes to the baking sheet. You should have roughly a dozen altogether. Lay half with the prettiest side down, cover with sliced cheese, and top the cheese with another pancake, prettiest side facing you. (If you're slipping in some serranos, green onions, or anything else, the time to do it is before you put the second pancake on.) Lay a large sheet of foil over the pancakes, and crimp the edges of the bottom sheet all around. Bake for 15 to 20 minutes or until the cheese is melted, and serve hot right from the oven.

TACOS DE CERDO EN SALSA ROJA
WITH AVOCADO-RADISH RELISH AND YELLOW RICE

SERVES 6 TO 8

Sometimes I want a saucy, spicy taco that can't be achieved with pulled pork. When I came up with this slow-cooked shoulder in red sauce I knew my call had been answered. A crowd-pleaser that's within any cook's reach, the recipe can be easily doubled. Be sure to have some queso fresco and Pico de Gallo (page 142) along with plenty of warm tortillas.

— TACOS DE CERDO EN SALSA ROJA —

3 LB/1.4 KG PORK SHOULDER, CUT INTO 1½-IN/4-CM CUBES

2 TO 5 TBSP ORGANIC HIGH-HEAT OIL (SEE HIGH-TEMPERATURE COOKING OILS, PAGE 17)

1 RED ONION, COARSELY CHOPPED

3 GARLIC CLOVES, CRUSHED

1 TBSP CUMIN SEED

1 TBSP CORIANDER SEED, LIGHTLY CRUSHED

1 TSP SMOKED PAPRIKA

8 CANNED SAN MARZANO TOMATOES, DRAINED, PLUS 1 CUP/240 ML OF THE JUICE

3 DRIED CHILES, SUCH AS PASILLA, STEMMED AND PARTIALLY SEEDED

3 CUPS/720 ML WATER OR CHICKEN STOCK

1 TSP KOSHER SALT

1 CUP/170 G CORN KERNELS, FRESH OR FROZEN

1 RED OR ORANGE BELL PEPPER, CUT INTO LARGE DICE

¼ CUP/10 G COARSELY CHOPPED FRESH CILANTRO

JUICE OF ½ LIME

FOR THE TABLE

¼ CUP/10 G COARSELY CHOPPED FRESH CILANTRO

20 CORN OR FLOUR TORTILLAS, WRAPPED TIGHTLY IN FOIL AND HEATED IN A 200°F/95°C OVEN

½ CUP/120 ML SOUR CREAM

In a large bowl, toss the meat with 1 to 2 tbsp of the oil to coat. Place your largest Dutch oven over medium-high heat, add 1 tbsp oil and, when it's hot, begin to brown the meat. Work in four to six batches, so as not to crowd the meat, turning and moving it around to brown on all sides. Transfer the browned meat to a plate as you work, and add more oil to the pot as needed. When all the meat is nicely browned and removed from the pan, turn off the heat and add the onion to the hot pot. Stir, add a little more oil if needed, and turn the heat on low. Cook, stirring often, for 5 to 6 minutes to soften. Add the garlic, cumin seed, coriander seed, and paprika and cook, stirring constantly, for 2 to 3 minutes. Add the juice from the tomatoes, stir, and turn off the heat.

Heat a cast-iron pan over high heat and roast the chiles until they are fragrant and lightly browned (a little black won't matter). Transfer the chiles to a blender, add the tomatoes, and work until smooth, 1 minute or so. Pour the tomato-chile blend into the pot and add the onion-spice mixture, the water, and salt. Add the browned meat, stir, and cover the pot tightly. Set over low heat and simmer gently for 3 hours, stirring occasionally. The stew should not dry out or scorch. Remove the lid to cook for the final hour, allowing some liquid to evaporate and leaving you with a thick, rich stew. Don't stir the pot too vigorously toward the end, or the meat will fall apart.

Preheat the oven to 400°F/200°C. Toss the corn and bell pepper with 1 or 2 tsp oil and lay out on a baking sheet. Roast for 12 to 14 minutes, or until black around the edges. Just before serving, add them to the pot along with the cilantro and the lime juice, and stir briefly. Serve with the chopped cilantro, warm tortillas, and sour cream. I like to put the pot of meat in the center of the table and pass the dishes around, letting everyone build their own taco. Double your taco and stuff it as full as you like.

— AVOCADO-RADISH RELISH —

One is crunchy, spicy, and fresh; the other rich, creamy, and decadent. Together, they're magnetic opposites that are much improved by the union—think Humphrey Bogart and Katharine Hepburn in *The African Queen*.

1 BUNCH CHERRY BELLE OR FRENCH BREAKFAST RADISHES, SOAKED BRIEFLY IN ICE WATER AND THINLY SLICED (ANY RADISH VARIETY WILL DO)

2 AVOCADOS, PITTED AND DICED

2 TBSP FRESH LIME JUICE

1 TSP KOSHER SALT

In a small bowl, combine the radishes, avocados, lime juice, and salt. Toss gently and serve.

— YELLOW RICE —

The subtle hint of sweetness from the onion combined with the heady scent of freshly toasted cumin seed satisfies two of your senses. The visual trick of the rich yellow delivered by the turmeric pleases the eye and makes this rice an asset to any meal.

2 TBSP BUTTER

1 ONION, CHOPPED

1 TSP GROUND TURMERIC

1 1/2 CUPS/310 G LONG-GRAIN RICE, RINSED

3 1/4 CUPS/770 ML WATER

KOSHER SALT

3 TSP CUMIN SEED, TOASTED

In a medium sauté pan set over medium heat, combine the butter, onion, and turmeric. Cook for 5 to 7 minutes, or until the onion is just softened. Transfer to a medium saucepan with a tight-fitting lid and add the rice, water, and 1 1/2 tsp salt. Cook, covered, over low heat for 20 to 22 minutes, or until the rice is tender and the water has evaporated.

While the rice cooks, heat the cumin seed very gently in a small cast-iron pan, toasting until fragrant, without burning. The lovely scent will tell you when it's done. When the rice is cooked, stir in the cumin seed, taste for salt, and serve.

TACOS AL PASTOR
WITH PINEAPPLE-ONION SALSA

SERVES 4

This taco has certain key elements of a classic al pastor—pineapple, onion, and pork—but I've moved the ingredients around and dispensed with the long marinating process as well as the spit cooking and subsequent shaving of the meat. Really, I've sneaked this recipe in because I like how the sweetness and acidity of the fruit works with the pork and onion. This is a big concession, as far as I'm concerned. Pineapple is the bimbo of the fruit world—too sweet and easy for my taste. When slow cooked with chiles and onion and slipped into a streamlined pulled pork taco, it discovers its true beauty and gains respectability. Make some margaritas with freshly squeezed lime juice and expensive tequila to bring the tropical flavors full circle. Of course, you'll never repent sides of Yellow Rice (page 137) and Miami Turtle Beans (page 122).

— TACOS AL PASTOR —

3 CUPS/660 G PULLED PORK (SEE CAROLINA PULLED PORK SANDWICH, PAGE 51)

12 TO 16 CORN TORTILLAS, 6 IN/15 CM IN DIAMETER

1 RECIPE PINEAPPLE-ONION SALSA (FACING PAGE)

1 CUP CHERRY BELLE RADISHES, SHREDDED

CILANTRO-TEQUILA CREMA (PAGE 143)

LIME WEDGES (MAKE PLENTY) FOR TACOS AND BEERS

FLAKY SALT FOR SERVING

HOT SAUCE FOR SERVING

Preheat the oven to 200°F/95°C. If the meat is cold, wrap it tightly in foil and put it in the oven for 15 to 20 minutes. Make two stacks of tortillas and seal in foil; heat for 10 to 15 minutes.

Put the salsa, radishes, crema, lime wedges, salt, and hot sauce on the table. When the meat and tortillas are hot, set them out and let people build their own tacos.

— PINEAPPLE-ONION SALSA —

This potent little concoction will transform your taco.

3 DRIED PASILLA OR GUAJILLO CHILES

2 TBSP OLIVE, PEANUT, OR VEGETABLE OIL

2 CUPS DICED FRESH PINEAPPLE

2 ONIONS, PREFERABLY VIDALIA, COARSELY CHOPPED

1 TBSP CUMIN SEED, TOASTED

3 GARLIC CLOVES, CHOPPED

Place the chiles in a small bowl and cover with hot water. Set aside to soak for at least 10 minutes, or up to 1 hour, before chopping. (If you want a less spicy salsa, don't add the seeds.)

In a large sauté pan set over low heat, combine the olive oil, pineapple, onions, cumin seed, garlic, and hydrated chiles. Cook, stirring frequently and scraping the bottom of the pan, for 25 to 30 minutes. The mixture should reduce and begin to brown, resulting in a dry salsa that looks more like what you might think of as a relish. Refrigerate for up to 1 day if not using right away.

ALL-IN PORK BURRITO
WITH GUACAMOLE, GREEN RICE, PICO DE GALLO, AND CILANTRO-TEQUILA CREMA

SERVES 4

A taste for this kind of classic California fast food is worth owning up to when you're really, seriously hungry—you know, those days when you forget to eat or when you've gone for an extra-long run and have used up every last resource your body has to offer.

The trick to success here is stuffing the tortilla as full as possible, without your greed causing the thing to break open. Learn as you work and, as with any composition with a dizzying range of ingredients, resist the urge to cheat on any seemingly minor parts.

— ALL-IN PORK BURRITO —

2 CUPS/400 G PULLED PORK (SEE CAROLINA PULLED PORK SANDWICH, PAGE 51)

KOSHER SALT

4 FLOUR TORTILLAS, 8 IN/20 CM IN DIAMETER

MIAMI TURTLE BEANS (PAGE 122), HOT

1/2 CUP/85 G CRUMBLED MEXICAN QUESO FRESCO

1 RECIPE GUACAMOLE (RECIPE FOLLOWS)

1 RECIPE GREEN RICE (PAGE 142)

1 RECIPE PICO DE GALLO (PAGE 142), DRAINED

2 LARGE ROMAINE LEAVES, CUT INTO FINE THREADS

1/4 CUP/10 G CILANTRO LEAVES

1 RECIPE CILANTRO-TEQUILA CREMA (PAGE 143)

HOT SAUCE (OPTIONAL)

Preheat the oven to 200°F/95°C. Season the meat with a little salt, as needed. If the meat is cold, wrap it tightly in aluminum foil and put it in the oven for 15 to 20 minutes. Wrap the tortillas in foil as well; heat for 10 to 15 minutes.

Set up an assembly line by first laying out the warm tortillas flat on the counter. Spread a line of beans across the center of each tortilla, leaving about a 1-in/2.5-cm border on the edge. Follow with a portion of pork, queso fresco, guacamole, rice, and pico de gallo. Add a few threads of lettuce for extra crunch, and an array of cilantro leaves, the crema, and an appropriate squiggle of hot sauce—or not, depending on whom you're cooking for.

Now comes the tricky part—bring the bottom edge of the tortilla up and over the filling, and then tuck it underneath the filling, rolling slightly as you tuck. While the tortilla is still partly open, tuck in the ends as well as you can by securing them inside the folded portion of the tortilla. Roll the rest of the way, keeping it as tight as possible, without losing all your ingredients out the sides. (Your ends may be coming undone, depending on how full the tortilla is. That's okay. It will be messy anyway.) You can wrap the burritos tightly in foil and return them to the hot oven briefly before serving, but don't leave them there long—the heat does no favors to the fresh ingredients.

— GUACAMOLE —

I believe in keeping it elemental when it comes to guacamole. Ripe avocados are the greatest gifts of nature—why mess up what's intrinsically perfect? If the people you cook for are anything like the people I cook for, you may want to double this recipe so you have plenty to eat with tortilla chips.

3 RIPE HASS AVOCADOS, PITTED AND FLESH SCOOPED FROM THE SKIN

JUICE OF 1 LIME, PLUS MORE AS NEEDED

KOSHER SALT

In a medium mixing bowl, combine the avocado, lime juice, and 1 tsp salt. Mash using either a potato masher, pastry cutter, or a fork until the mixture is smooth. Taste for salt and acid, adding additional salt or lime juice as needed—the guacamole should taste of avocado, not lime. If you're working ahead, scrape down the sides of the bowl, squeeze a few drops of lime juice on the surface of the guacamole, and, without stirring, press plastic wrap down directly on the surface of the guacamole, leaving none of it exposed to the air. This keeps for 1 day at most.

— GREEN RICE —

Pretty and flavorful, this green rice is as much a pleasure to look at as it is to eat. Use it for any Latin dish, but be sure to double or even triple the recipe, as this makes just the right amount to stuff four fat burritos.

½ CUP/105 G LONG-GRAIN BASMATI RICE, RINSED AND DRAINED

1 CUP/240 ML WATER

¼ TSP KOSHER SALT

1 TBSP BUTTER

¼ CUP/10 G FINELY CHOPPED FRESH CILANTRO

Combine the rice, water, and salt in a small saucepan with a tight-fitting lid. Set over medium heat and cook, covered, for 12 to 15 minutes, or until the water has evaporated and the rice is tender.

Combine the butter and cilantro in another small saucepan and set over low heat. Once the butter is melted, pour the mixture over the rice and combine with a fork. Cover to keep the rice hot until serving.

— PICO DE GALLO —

The colors—flaming orange peppers, canary-yellow mangoes, crimson tomatoes, and grassy green onions—make a tempting, redolent salsa. It does honor to everything from chips to meat to rice, so spread it around generously.

1 LARGE TOMATO, FINELY DICED

6 GREEN ONIONS, TRIMMED TOP AND BOTTOM AND THINLY SLICED (USE IT ALL)

1 MANGO, PEELED AND FINELY CHOPPED

½ SERRANO CHILE, MINCED, WITH SEEDS

¼ ORANGE BELL PEPPER, SEEDED, MEMBRANE REMOVED, AND FINELY DICED

½ CUP/85 G FRESH CORN KERNELS, SHAVED OFF THE COB (OMIT IF IT'S NOT CORN SEASON)

½ TSP BEST OLIVE OIL (SEE OLIVE OIL, PAGE 18)

1 TSP FRESH LIME JUICE

½ TSP KOSHER SALT

In a small mixing bowl, combine the tomato, green onions, mango, serrano, bell pepper, corn (if using), olive oil, and lime juice. Mix well. Just before serving, pour off any liquid that may have accumulated in the bowl, and stir in the salt.

— CILANTRO-TEQUILA CREMA —

Straight-up crema is an excellent addition to virtually any Latin meal. This recipe brings complexity to the cooling, mellow qualities that make it such a welcome contrast to spicy food.

1 CUP/240 ML CREMA
(SUBSTITUTE FULL-FAT SOUR CREAM)

2 TBSP TEQUILA

2 TSP FRESH LIME JUICE

1 BUNCH CILANTRO STEMS WITH A FEW LEAVES
STILL ATTACHED (OR NOT)

Combine the crema, tequila, lime juice, and cilantro stems in a blender and work until smooth. Serve chilled.

MAYAN POC CHUC,
SLOW-COOKED RED ONIONS, AND
CITRUS-AVOCADO SALAD

SERVES 4

It's difficult to surpass the pleasures of exploring the stunning
Tulum ruins, perched on the cliff along the eastern coast of
the Yucatán Peninsula. You can give it a shot this way: Follow
your tour by making your way down the steep steps, hot and
sweaty after witnessing the ancient marvels, peeling off your
clothes, stowing them on a rock, and plunging into the ocean for
a long cooling float in the waves. My idea of balance? A solid
appreciation of the magnificent ancient Mayan culture and then
some serious time beaching it. This dish is a classic Yucatán
creation, in keeping with the spirit of both self-indulgence and
Mayan culture. Traditional versions of *poc chuc* are made with sour
oranges, something I can never find. I've substituted other citrus
here. Thick, bone-in ham steaks are a lovely cut, with plenty of
rich, dark meat, rimmed with tasty fat. The Citrus-Avocado Salad
combines the vast virtues of a silky avocado with additional
citrus. Serve with the Slow-Cooked Red Onions and maybe a big bowl
of Yellow Rice (page 137). A fresh lime margarita will complete
the full vacation experience.

— MAYAN POC CHUC —

1 OR 2 BONE-IN FRESH HAM STEAKS,
ABOUT 1 IN/2.5 CM THICK
(1½ TO 3 LB/680 G TO 1.4 KG TOTAL;
SUBSTITUTE SHOULDER, RIB, OR
LOIN CHOPS)

1 TSP KOSHER SALT

JUICE OF 2 LIMES

JUICE OF 1 LEMON

JUICE OF 2 ORANGES OR TANGERINES

Lay the ham steak in a glass baking dish and rub with the salt.
Add the lime juice, lemon juice, and orange juice to the dish and
turn the meat a few times to coat. Set the meat to marinate for

1 hour on the counter, or up to 24 hours in the refrigerator. (Be sure to rest the meat at room temperature to take the chill off before cooking, if you marinate in the refrigerator.)

Build a medium fire in a charcoal or wood grill or heat a gas grill to medium. If you're using charcoal or wood, you want hot embers, not flames. Use a clean, well-cured grate.

Preheat the oven to 200°F/95°C. Place the meat over the coals and watch carefully for flare-ups, flipping frequently. Get some good color, with a little black on the fat and nice brown color on the meat—this will take 8 to 10 minutes. You'll need to watch the meat and turn it often, as the fat will cause flare-ups. As it cooks, the sides of the steak will curl up, creating a sort of bowl, where the meat juices will accumulate. Don't dump the juices or flip the meat. Continue cooking, allowing the juices to accumulate, for 12 to 15 minutes. Watch carefully; the cooking time depends on the intensity of your fire and the temperature outdoors. The meat is done when the accumulated juices lose most of their pinkness. When the meat appears done (cut into it near the bone if necessary), place on a platter and finish it in the oven for 5 minutes. It should reach no less than 145°F/63°C on an instant-read thermometer inserted at the thickest point, near the bone. Carve the steak into long strips and serve.

— SLOW-COOKED RED ONIONS —

Most people are apt to throw half an onion facedown on the grill to soften and char lightly while their meat cooks. It makes sense. I do it, too. But those soft, lightly charred onions are even better broken apart and tossed with salt and a splash of vinegar. That's what you'll discover here, enlivened by chopped parsley and black pepper. If you're cooking *poc chuc*, put the onions on as soon as your fire is built; they can take up to 2 hours, depending on the heat of your fire.

3 LARGE RED ONIONS, HALVED AT THE EQUATOR, SKIN ON

1 TBSP ORGANIC HIGH-HEAT OIL (SEE HIGH-TEMPERATURE COOKING OILS, PAGE 17)

1 TSP KOSHER SALT

2 TEASPOONS CIDER VINEGAR

1/4 CUP/10 G PARSLEY

BLACK PEPPER

Coat the cut faces of the onions with the oil and place, cut-side down, over indirect heat on the grill. Cook, moving the onion halves around only to ensure that each one is getting optimal heat, for 1½ to 2 hours. They should be lightly charred on the edge and very soft. Transfer the onions to a bowl, remove the skins and any tough outer layers, and use kitchen scissors to snip the largest pieces and to remove the stem. Toss with the salt, vinegar, parsley, and a grind of black pepper. Serve warm.

— CITRUS-AVOCADO SALAD —

Avocado combined with an array of citrus makes this an ideal winter salad. Think December through March, the height of citrus season in California, Texas, and Florida. When cutting the fruit, be sure to work on an immaculate surface—place a bit of parchment on the cutting surface before starting if you're uncertain. Residual garlic or onion flavor will mar this fresh, bright salad.

3 AVOCADOS, PITTED AND SLICED

1 TSP FRESH LIME JUICE

GRATED ZEST OF ½ ORGANIC LEMON (MEYER, IF YOU CAN GET IT), PLUS 1 TSP OF THE JUICE

3 ORGANIC TANGERINES OR SATSUMA MANDARINS, CUT INTO SUPREMES (PEELED, SEGMENTED, MEMBRANE REMOVED), PLUS THE GRATED ZEST OF ½ TANGERINE OR SATSUMA MANDARIN

1 CARA CARA ORANGE, CUT INTO SUPREMES (PEELED, SEGMENTED, MEMBRANE REMOVED)

1 PINK GRAPEFRUIT, CUT INTO SUPREMES (PEELED, SEGMENTED, MEMBRANE REMOVED)

1 TBSP BEST OLIVE OIL (SEE OLIVE OIL, PAGE 18)

FLAKY OR COARSE SALT AND BLACK PEPPER FOR FINISHING

In a large mixing bowl, toss the avocados with the lime juice and lemon juice. Sprinkle with the lemon zest and tangerine zest. Add the tangerine, Cara Cara, and grapefruit supremes. A drizzle of olive oil, a pinch of salt, and a grind of black pepper are all the dressing this dashing salad needs before serving.

"EAT, PRAY, LOVE" FEIJOADA COMPLETA FOR A CROWD,
WITH SIDES AND CONDIMENTS

SERVES 30

The fairy-tale romance that winds down my dear friend Elizabeth Gilbert's memoir, *Eat, Pray, Love*, was due in no small part to this magnificent stew. Then again, Jose himself, the man who happened to cook it for a party at a friend's house in Bali, where the two first met, is pretty magnificent himself. I confess, it's difficult for me to imagine feijoada without Jose's bubbly, cheerful generosity. Every time I've had his feijoada, it's been a little different. Then again, Jose has never written the recipe down. Like most good cooks, he works by instinct, having learned all he needed to know by watching his mother, Altair, regularly make it at home in Porto Alegre, Brazil, where he grew up. Whether you're aiming to seduce or seriously impress, this dish has a particular magic to it that delivers unseen wonders. Just ask Liz.

— "EAT, PRAY, LOVE" FEIJOADA COMPLETA — FOR A CROWD

1 1/8 LB/510 G PORK BELLY

6 OZ/170 G BACON, CUBED, PLUS
6 OZ/170 G SKIN FROM SLAB BACON

5 LB/2.3 KG DRIED BLACK TURTLE BEANS, SOAKED
FOR 8 TO 12 HOURS, AND WATER CHANGED TWICE
(THIS IS HOW JOSE DOES IT)

3 LB/1.4 KG SMOKED HAM HOCKS

2 TBSP BLACK PEPPERCORNS

1/4 CUP/5 G DRIED OREGANO

1/4 CUP/5 G DRIED PARSLEY

3 PIG'S TROTTERS, SPLIT

2 PIG'S EARS

3 TBSP CORIANDER SEED, COARSELY GROUND WITH
A MORTAR AND PESTLE OR SPICE GRINDER

1 1/2 LB/680 G SMOKED PORK BUTT,
CUT INTO LARGE CHUNKS

1 LB/455 G ROLLED PANCETTA,
CUT INTO LONG STRIPS

1 LB/455 G HAM, CUT INTO LARGE CHUNKS

2 LB/910 G NECK BONES

2 LB/910 G SHOULDER MEAT, SUCH AS PORK BUTT,
CUT INTO LARGE CHUNKS

2 ONIONS, HALVED AND THINLY SLICED

1 HEAD GARLIC, CLOVES CRUSHED, PEELED,
AND COARSELY CHOPPED

3 TOMATOES, COARSELY CHOPPED

3 TO 3 1/2 LB/1.4 TO 1.6 KG SPARERIBS
(RAW OR COOKED AND SMOKED), CUT APART
INTO SINGLE RIBS

24 GREEN ONIONS, TRIMMED TOP AND BOTTOM
(USE IT ALL), HALF CHOPPED AND
HALF THINLY SLICED

3/4 CUP/30 G CHOPPED FRESH OREGANO

8 OZ/225 G BOAR SAUSAGE, CUT INTO CHUNKS
(SUBSTITUTE SPICY OR MILD PORK SAUSAGE
OF ANY KIND)

1 1/3 LB/605 G BRATWURST, CUT INTO THIRDS

1 LB/455 G BREAKFAST SAUSAGE

1 CUP/40 G CHOPPED FRESH CILANTRO

2 CUPS/80 G CHOPPED FRESH PARSLEY

KOSHER SALT (IF NEEDED)

Cube 6 oz/170 g of the pork belly and set the rest aside. In a large cast-iron frying pan set over low heat, combine the cubed pork belly and bacon. Cook, stirring often, for 15 to 20 minutes, or until the cubes are crispy and about 1 cup/240 ml of fat has been rendered. Turn down the heat if the fat smokes. Pour the fat off and set aside. (Transfer the cracklings to a plate and set aside to use for the Bacon-Banana Farofa.)

Reserve 1 lb/455 g of the beans. Put the remaining 4 lb/1.8 g beans in a large stockpot and add enough water to cover them by 3 in/7.5 cm. Bring the water to a boil over high heat, turn down the heat, and add the ham hocks, peppercorns, dried oregano, and dried parsley. Cover and simmer for 1 hour, skimming any scum that rises to the surface. Add the bacon skin, the remaining 12 oz/340 g pork belly, the trotters, and ears. Keep the pot covered and simmer for another

2 hours, stirring occasionally. Remove the hocks, trotters, and ears from the pot. Remove the skin and meat from the bones and cut the meat into chunks (allow to cool briefly or use a knife and fork to work with the hot meat). Discard the bones. Add the reserved 1 lb/455 g beans to the pot along with the cubed cooked meat, the ground coriander seed, smoked butt, pancetta, ham, neck bones, and shoulder meat. Cover and simmer for 1 hour more.

Heat the reserved pork fat in a large sauté pan over medium heat. Add the onions, garlic, and tomatoes and cook for 8 to 12 minutes, or until the onions are soft. Add the onion mixture to the pot. Wipe out the sauté pan and add the spareribs. Brown the ribs for 12 to 15 minutes and add them to the pot. Add the chopped green onions, fresh oregano, boar sausage, bratwurst, and breakfast sausage. Cover and simmer for 1 hour before adding the cilantro and half the parsley. Put the remaining half of the parsley in a bowl with the sliced green onions to serve on the side. Fill a blender with 2 cups/420 g hot liquidy beans scooped from the bottom of the pot and work until smooth. Return to the pot and repeat with another 2 cups/420 g of beans.

Taste the feijoada. You should not have added any salt and it's likely that the stew will not need any, given all the cured and salted meats, but check just to be sure. The pancetta, shoulder meat, and ribs should be very soft, and the meat should be coming off the rib bones. Cook, uncovered, for another 20 to 30 minutes if the stew is too thin. Transfer the feijoada to a serving pot and bring it to the table with a ladle. Serve with the parsley-green onion mixture.

— SIDES AND CONDIMENTS —

ORANGE SEGMENTS

This is an elemental component, adding a bright, sweet note—and a
dimension of color—to your plate.

12 NAVEL ORANGES, CUT INTO SUPREMES
(PEELED, SEGMENTED, MEMBRANE REMOVED)

¼ CUP/10 G CHOPPED FRESH PARSLEY

Put the orange segments in a large bowl and sprinkle with the
parsley before serving.

BACON-BANANA FAROFA

Farofa (manioc flour), toasted in butter with bananas and bacon, is
a component of feijoada that's not to be missed. The crumb absorbs
the soupy bean liquid, mixing with the salsa and the juice from the
oranges on your plate to bring the whole into harmonic sync.

½ CUP/115 G BUTTER

1 ONION, CHOPPED

3 GARLIC CLOVES, CHOPPED

2 RIPE BANANAS, CUT INTO SMALL CHUNKS

2½ CUPS/300 G *FAROFA*

2 TSP *AZEITE DE DENDÊ* (PALM OIL, OPTIONAL),
OR RENDERED PORK FAT

CRACKLINGS FROM 6 OZ/170 G PORK BELLY AND
6 OZ/170 G BACON (RESERVED FROM THE FEIJOADA)

Add the butter to a large sauté pan, and set over medium heat. When
the butter melts, add the onion and cook for 3 to 5 minutes, or
until soft. Add the garlic and bananas and cook for another 2 to
3 minutes before adding the *farofa*, *azeite de dendê* (if using),
and the cracklings. Cook for 8 to 10 minutes, stirring frequently,
until lightly toasted. The *farofa* should be hot and ever so
faintly browned. Transfer to a plate and serve.

PIMENTA MALAGUETA BEAN SAUCE

This surprisingly spicy sauce looks a lot like refried beans, with a smooth, lovely heat to match. It's one of my favorite hot sauces. If you can't find jarred *pimenta malagueta*, use a few habañeros. The sauce is meant to be bracingly spicy.

2 CUPS/420 G HOT LIQUIDY BEANS FROM THE FEIJOADA POT

¼ CUP/60 ML *PIMENTA MALAGUETA* OIL

8 TO 10 *PIMENTA MALAGUETA*, WITH THEIR LIQUID

Remove the beans from the bottom of the feijoada pot (and possibly a little skin or boneless meat) and put it in a blender with the oil. Work until smooth, and transfer to a bowl. Add the chiles and their liquid, stir, and taste (it should be very spicy) before serving.

JOSE'S MILD SALSA

You'll want to have plenty of this fresh, surprisingly mild salsa. Like the oranges, it brightens the plate, providing acidity and subtle heat.

2 ONIONS, CHOPPED

3 TOMATOES, CHOPPED

5 JALAPEÑOS, CHOPPED, HALF OF THEM SEEDED

1 CUP/240 ML WHITE VINEGAR

1 CUP/240 ML ORGANIC REFINED OLIVE OIL (SEE OLIVE OIL, PAGE 18)

½ CUP/20 G CHOPPED FRESH PARSLEY

½ CUP/20 G CHOPPED FRESH CILANTRO

1 TSP KOSHER SALT

Combine the onions, tomatoes, jalapeños, vinegar, olive oil, parsley, cilantro, and salt in a medium bowl. Cover and refrigerate for at least 2 hours, or up to 24 hours, before serving.

KALE WITH BACON, ONIONS, AND GARLIC

As if you need more pork. Well, maybe you do, because the kale goes fast with a crowd. Make more, if you like, by working in batches. You could also use collards rather than kale if you prefer.

6 OZ/170 G BACON, CUBED

1 ONION, DICED

1 TSP KOSHER SALT

3 GARLIC CLOVES, MINCED

5 LB/2.3 KG KALE, WASHED AND CUT INTO RIBBONS (YOU WANT THE MOISTURE ON THE LEAVES)

Cook the bacon gently in a large sauté pan or wok set over medium-low heat, 8 to 10 minutes, stirring frequently. Add the onion and salt and cook in the bacon fat with the bacon for another 1 to 2 minutes. Stir in the garlic, just heating it, before adding the kale. Work in batches, or add as much kale as you can, using tongs to turn it, and adding more to the pan as the leaves wilt and lose volume. Cook, turning frequently, until just tender, and serve.

BASMATI RICE

This recipe makes a huge pot of rice—but you have a gigantic pot of feijoada, so you'll probably need it.

5 CUPS/930 G BASMATI RICE, RINSED AND DRAINED

11 CUPS/2.6 L WATER

1/4 CUP/60 ML ORGANIC REFINED OLIVE OIL (SEE OLIVE OIL, PAGE 18)

3 GREEN ONIONS, TRIMMED TOP AND BOTTOM AND CHOPPED (USE IT ALL)

Combine the rice, water, olive oil, and green onions in a medium pot with a tight-fitting lid. Cook over medium-low heat for 15 to 20 minutes. (Add additional water if needed, or remove the lid and allow the rice to dry out briefly for the last few minutes if it's tender but too wet.) Fluff with a fork and serve.

CAIPIRINHA

As you spend your afternoon cooking, you're sure to gather a
crowd. Make a few batches of Caipirinhas to keep the cook and
guests happy as the kitchen gets busy. It will take the edge off
as the crowd grows hungrier right on cue, as the tempting scent
of feijoada fills the air.

1 LIME, PLUS 1 LIME WEDGE, NOTCHED	2 TSP SUGAR
2½ OZ/75 ML CACHAÇA	ICE CUBES

Peel half the lime with a vegetable peeler. Quarter the lime, and
combine with the lime peel, cachaça, and sugar in a cocktail shaker.
Work the lime with a muddler (a pestle will do) to extract the juice
and some pith. Add an ice cube, cover tightly, and shake like you
mean it. (Really, hold the shaker over your head and shake hard
until your arms are tired.) Pour through a cocktail strainer over
a glass or pitcher half filled with ice. Serve with the notched
lime wedge on the edge of the glass.

CHINESE AND JAPANESE PORK

CHINESE AND JAPANESE PORK

The ingredients I call for in this chapter are challenging, but only if you don't have a Japanese, Chinese, or Korean supermarket nearby or access to the great shopping mall that is the World Wide Web. I like AsianSupermarket365.com if I really need something, because they carry a wide variety of condiments, noodles, and dried ingredients, all in one place. I prefer, of course, to spend hours dazed, wandering the aisles of one of the football field-size Asian supermarkets in my area, piling my cart high with ingredients both familiar and bizarre to my Western eyes.

Here are the basics you'll need for cooking the food in this chapter, other than Sriracha sauce, fresh ginger, cilantro, and *mae ploy* (sweet chile sauce), which every corner store sells these days. A fresh, dated bag of jasmine rice and plenty of light and dark soy sauce, including the dark mushroom soy from Pearl River Bridge, which I'm so addicted to, are fairly obvious. Among the slightly more exotic items, you'll want mirin, Shaoxing cooking wine, chile paste (Lao Luo Zi brand's Chaotian Chili King is my favorite), chile bean paste (look for the same brand), shrimp paste, chile shrimp paste, dried shrimp, dashi flakes, dashi miso paste, rice vinegar, Chinkiang vinegar, ramen noodles, soba and various rice and mung bean noodles, Sichuan peppercorns, hoisin sauce, toasted sesame oil, and pickled ginger. Of course, you can buy only what you need for a single recipe, rather than buying every ingredient listed here. Explore, experiment, and have fun with these wildly flavorful, intense ingredients.

DRINKS

I'm drinking more beer lately, and when it comes to Asian recipes
with spice and a heavy umami component, beer makes more sense than
wine or cocktails. If you prefer to skip the booze, hot or cold tea
naturally suits the foods in this chapter. Aside from the obvious
green tea, try roasted barley tea, served cold. It's caffeine-free
and refreshing all on its own, with a clean, pleasing toasty flavor
that's a lot like the Japanese roasted rice and green tea combination, called *genmaicha*, which is fairly common in the United States.

ON THE TABLE

Chopsticks slow my pace enough that I seem to enjoy my food more.
They make sense for the recipes here, for the most part. Be sure to
put the soy sauce on the table along with salt and some of that
ubiquitous Sriracha as well. Small plates and little bowls of
condiments and greens go with the spirit of a Chinese meal, which
is often shared, rather than doled out individually, with lots
of passing and grabbing and requesting going on to enliven the
table. I'm thinking green onions, chiles, and pickles.

SWEETS

Green tea ice cream, macaroons with a hint of anise, or a simple
custard flavored with a dot of pure almond extract aren't traditional, but they are delicious and feel right with the recipes
in this chapter. I find the world of Japanese desserts more inter-
esting than Chinese desserts, if only because they're so foreign
to me and so magically precise. I'm thinking of the exotic adzuki
bean puddings and little cakes so intricately composed, they
surpass all but the best sushi masters' attention to detail.

PORK FRIED RICE

SERVES 4

When you're thinking, "Let's do takeout" because you can't banish
the too-rich and too-salty but deeply satisfying taste of fried
rice from your memory, this recipe is your salvation. Made right,
fried rice is delightfully rich but need not be so greasy you
could light it on fire—I suspect many Chinese takeout versions
are indeed flammable. One bite of this version—with more umami
than salt, and loaded with vegetables, pork, and egg, with a whiff
of sausage sneaked in for depth of flavor—and you'll be throwing
that ratty takeout menu in the trash. (As for your craving for
fried rice, that may not be disposed of so easily.) Be sure to dice
every ingredient small—the size of peas if peas were square.
It's tedious but worth the trouble.

1½ CUPS/285 G JASMINE RICE, RINSED AND DRAINED, OR 3 CUPS/310 G DAY-OLD COOKED RICE

2 CUPS/480 ML WATER

1 LB/455 G BONE-IN SHOULDER CHOP, DICED (CENTER-CUT; BONELESS TENDS TO BE TOO LEAN)

1 TBSP PEELED AND GRATED FRESH GINGER

2 TBSP SOY SAUCE, PLUS MORE FOR SERVING

1 TBSP FISH SAUCE

2 TBSP CHINESE COOKING WINE (THE DARK SHAOXING IS IDEAL)

1 SERRANO CHILE, MINCED

2 TBSP ORGANIC HIGH-HEAT OIL (SEE HIGH-TEMPERATURE COOKING OILS, PAGE 17)

3 OZ/85 G SWEET OR SPICY PORK SAUSAGE, REMOVED FROM THE CASING

3 TBSP BUTTER

6 EGGS

6 LARGE GREEN BEANS, TRIMMED AND DICED

3 CARROTS, PEELED AND DICED

5 MUSHROOMS, TRIMMED AND DICED (SHIITAKES ARE MY FAVORITE, BUT ANY KIND WILL DO)

1 CUP/115 G PEAS, FRESH OR FROZEN

6 GREEN ONIONS, TRIMMED TOP AND BOTTOM AND THINLY SLICED (USE IT ALL)

¼ CUP/10 G CHOPPED FRESH PARSLEY

1 TBSP TOASTED SESAME OIL, PLUS MORE FOR SERVING

10 BABY SPINACH LEAVES, CUT INTO RIBBONS

¼ CUP/10 G SNIPPED FRESH CHIVES

HOT SAUCE FOR SERVING

Preheat the oven to 180°F/80°C. Combine the rice and water in a medium
saucepan set over high heat. Bring to a boil, cover tightly, and
cook for 8 to 12 minutes, or until the water evaporates. (The water-
to-rice ratio here is intentionally low so that the rice will be

harder and less cooked.) Spread out the rice on a baking sheet and place it in the oven to dry for 15 to 20 minutes, flipping the rice once midway through the cooking time. (Skip this step if you have day-old cooked rice.)

In a medium bowl, stir together the pork, ginger, soy sauce, fish sauce, cooking wine, and chile. Set aside. Heat a wok or a large cast-iron frying pan over high heat until it begins to smoke. Add 1 tbsp of the high-heat oil and the sausage (careful of spatters!), stirring constantly to break up the sausage, which you want in small bits, not large cooked clumps. After about 1 min-ute, when the sausage is no longer pink, add the pork along with all its sauces. Cook for 3 to 5 minutes over high heat, running it up the side of the wok with a slotted spoon or wok skimmer until it's cooked through. (You don't want to steam it!) Transfer the meat to a plate, leaving the juices behind.

Melt the butter in a sauté pan over medium-low heat. When the butter is hot, crack 4 of the eggs into the pan and cook, sliding a spatula under each one once it's set to be sure it's not sticking. Don't flip the eggs. Instead, baste them with a little of the butter to cook the whites. Set aside off the heat once the whites are mostly set and the yolks are still runny.

Add the remaining 1 tbsp high-heat oil to the wok, heat over high heat, and add the green beans, carrots, mushrooms, and peas. Cook, running the vegetables up the side as you did the meat, for 4 to 5 minutes, or until the liquid in the bottom of the wok evaporates and the vegetables begin to stick to the wok. Transfer to a plate (with the meat if you like), leaving behind any liquid or oil to finish the eggs.

Beat the remaining 2 eggs in a small bowl. Holding the wok off the heat for a moment, add the green onions and parsley and, right on top of that, the beaten eggs. Return the wok to high heat and stir once or twice with a rubber spatula, tilting the wok to expose more of the egg to the heat while scraping the egg from the sides and the bottom of the wok. While you still have plenty of uncooked egg, add the rice. Stir once or twice, scraping the wok and mashing the rice to coat it with the egg. Return the meat and vegetables to the wok and add the sesame oil. Stir for 1 or 2 minutes, scraping the bottom of the wok frequently. Add the spinach, stirring it into the rice just to wilt it. Serve in pasta bowls with a fried egg on top of each serving, and finish with a sprinkle of chives. Bring hot sauce, soy sauce, and toasted sesame oil to pass at the table, although I doubt you'll need them.

BRAISED COUNTRY RIBS IN LEMONGRASS-ANISE STOCK

SERVES 4

The magic of watching a big pot of aromatics and raw, bony meat transform itself into a fragrant, delicious stew is one of the most gratifying aspects of cooking. Try this recipe out some wintery day, and see if the results don't make you feel like a sorcerer. Despite the litany of ingredients, this is a recipe to make when you don't have time to fuss over dinner. Once you brown the meat in the oven and get it on the stove, you can do something else while it bubbles away for the next half hour, reminding you of its progress only through its irresistible scent.

3 TO 3½ LB/1.4 TO 1.6 KG COUNTRY RIBS (OR USE BONE-IN SLICED SHOULDER OR SPARERIBS)

3 TBSP ORGANIC HIGH-HEAT OIL (SEE HIGH-TEMPERATURE COOKING OILS, PAGE 17)

6 OZ/170 G BEECH MUSHROOMS, TRIMMED AND LEFT WHOLE (SUBSTITUTE SHIITAKES OR CREMINI, THINLY SLICED)

1 ONION, CHOPPED

5 GARLIC CLOVES, SLICED

3 DRIED TIENTSIN CHILES OR OTHER HOT DRIED CHILES

8 CUPS/2 L WATER

ONE 3-IN/7.5-CM PIECE FRESH GINGER, PEELED AND THINLY SLICED

3 STAR ANISE PODS, BROKEN INTO PIECES

⅓ CUP/35 G THINLY SLICED LEMONGRASS (ABOUT 2 STALKS, TENDER PART ONLY)

2 YAMS, PEELED AND CUT INTO BITE-SIZE CHUNKS

1 TURNIP, PEELED AND CUT INTO BITE-SIZE CHUNKS

1 CUP/195 G DRIED ADZUKI BEANS

¼ CUP/60 ML SHAOXING COOKING WINE

2 TBSP SOY SAUCE (DARK IF YOU HAVE IT)

KOSHER SALT

8 GREEN ONIONS, TRIMMED TOP AND BOTTOM AND THINLY SLICED (USE IT ALL)

2 TBSP FRESH LEMON JUICE

ONE 6-OZ/170-G PACKAGE SOBA (BUCKWHEAT NOODLES), COOKED ACCORDING TO PACKAGE DIRECTIONS, DRAINED, AND RINSED

Preheat the oven to 400°F/200°C. Dry the meat and coat it all over with 1 tbsp of the oil. Place the meat on a baking sheet so the pieces aren't touching. Roast for 20 minutes before turning the pieces over and roasting for another 20 minutes. The meat should be nicely browned and will have rendered some of its fat.

While the meat browns, heat 1 tbsp oil in a large Dutch oven (12 in/ 30.5 cm in diameter) over high heat. Add the mushrooms and cook for 3 to 4 minutes, until just wilted and lightly fragrant. Transfer to a plate and set aside. Without washing the pot, add the remaining 1 tbsp oil along with the onion and sauté for 3 to 4 minutes over medium heat. Add the garlic and chiles and cook, stirring frequently, for another 3 to 4 minutes, reducing the heat further if the garlic begins to brown. Add the water, ginger, star anise, lemongrass, yams, turnip, and adzuki beans. Set the pot, uncovered, over medium heat. Once the liquid boils, turn the heat to low and simmer. Add the meat to the pot, leaving any extra fat behind. All the ingredients should be submerged or nearly so. Cook for 1 hour before adding the cooking wine, soy sauce, and 1½ tsp salt. Continue to cook the stew for another 20 to 30 minutes, or just until the beans are tender and the stock has thickened slightly to become a rich broth. Stir in the reserved mushrooms along with the green onions and lemon juice. Taste for salt and serve over the buckwheat noodles.

SICHUAN PEPPER-RUBBED RIBS
WITH GINGERED SNAP PEAS

SERVES 4

Sichuan pepper is like nothing else as it tingles and smarts on your tongue, awakening every sense. I find the sensation irresistible. These ribs aren't too spicy, but you will taste the outstanding and unusual flavor of this complex rub, with its hint of fermented black beans, which deliver a depth of flavor I don't know how to match with any other ingredient. The Gingered Snap Peas are a refreshing, simple antidote to the peppery ribs. To finish the plate, a big pot of Jasmine Rice (page 185) would be ideal.

— SICHUAN PEPPER-RUBBED RIBS —

4 TO 5 LB/1.8 TO 2.3 KG ST. LOUIS-CUT RIBS OR SPARERIBS (2 OR 3 SLABS), SILVERSKIN REMOVED (SEE THE INSTRUCTIONS ON PAGE 15)

2 TBSP PEANUT OR VEGETABLE OIL

2 TBSP SICHUAN PEPPERCORNS

1 TBSP GREEN PEPPERCORNS

1 TBSP BLACK PEPPERCORNS

2 TBSP KOSHER SALT

1 TBSP FERMENTED BLACK BEANS

6 GREEN ONIONS, TRIMMED TOP AND BOTTOM AND SLICED INTO THIN ROUNDS (USE IT ALL)

Lay the ribs out on two baking sheets and coat on both sides with the peanut oil. Combine the Sichuan peppercorns, green peppercorns, black peppercorns, salt, and fermented black beans in a spice grinder or mortar. Coarsely grind the peppercorns and black beans—they should be about the consistency of kosher salt. Coat the ribs on both sides with the spice mixture.

Preheat the oven to 225°F/110°C. (If you prefer to grill, see instructions on page 39.) Roast the ribs for 3 to 3½ hours, flipping them halfway through the cooking time. They're done when they're nicely browned, crispy on the outside, and falling-off-the-bone tender. Pile them on a platter, scatter the green onions on top, and serve.

— GINGERED SNAP PEAS —

Lime, ginger, coconut, and peas are a surprising combination. Quick and bright, this is a recipe for early winter, when snap peas are the only fresh vegetable you can find that hasn't been flown in from another continent.

2 TBSP VIRGIN COCONUT OIL (SUBSTITUTE ORGANIC HIGH-HEAT OIL; SEE HIGH-TEMPERATURE COOKING OILS, PAGE 17)

12 OZ/340 G SUGAR SNAP PEAS

1 TBSP PEELED AND FINELY GRATED FRESH GINGER

JUICE OF 1 LIME

¼ TSP KOSHER SALT

FLAKY SALT (OPTIONAL)

In a large sauté pan set over medium heat, warm the coconut oil, and then add the snap peas, ginger, lime juice, and kosher salt. Cook, stirring and scraping the bottom of the pan frequently, until the peas are hot and have lost their raw flavor, 6 to 8 minutes. Transfer to a bowl, taste, and add a pinch of flaky salt (if they need it) before serving.

KOWLOON RIBS,
SESAME BROCCOLI, AND
DRIED SHRIMP RICE

SERVES 4

Happily will I admit to gobbling the lowly, bright-red ribs I find on my threshold—along with steaming dumplings and funky mai fun—when I order Chinese takeout or find myself seated at the table pointing at everything that passes by for a Hong Kong-style dim sum pig-out. I've duplicated those ribs here, sans dye. Even if they won't glow like the grenadine cloud at the bottom of a Shirley Temple, they'll be damn fine whether you get some smoke on them in your grill or cook them low and slow in the oven.

— KOWLOON RIBS —

4 TO 5 LB/1.8 TO 2.3 KG ST. LOUIS-CUT RIBS OR SPARERIBS (2 OR 3 SLABS), SILVERSKIN REMOVED (SEE THE INSTRUCTIONS ON PAGE 15) AND CUT APART INTO SINGLE RIBS

1/4 CUP/60 ML VINEGAR

2 TBSP HOISIN SAUCE

1/4 CUP/60 ML SOY SAUCE

2 TBSP PEANUT OR VEGETABLE OIL

4 GARLIC CLOVES, CRUSHED

1 TBSP CHINESE FIVE-SPICE POWDER

1 TSP KOSHER SALT

PLENTY OF BLACK PEPPER

Place the ribs in a large mixing bowl. Combine the remaining ingredients in a blender and blend until smooth, about 1 minute. Pour the mixture over the ribs and turn the ribs to coat all over. Set aside to marinate on the counter for 1 hour, or refrigerate for up to 24 hours.

Preheat the oven to 225°F/110°C. (If you prefer to grill, see the instructions on page 39.) Lay the ribs on two baking sheets, spreading them out so that they don't touch. Cook for 2½ to 3 hours, flipping the ribs once halfway through the cooking time. The ribs should be falling-off-the-bone tender and crispy on the outside. Put them on a platter and serve.

— SESAME BROCCOLI —

My friend Kazumi Futagawa, a gifted and extraordinarily precise cook, is always bringing some delicacy she has concocted at home into the kitchen where we work together—outrageous pickles, soba noodles with dashi, barley tea. One day, she made a version of this recipe right in the kitchen, passing it around for everyone to share. I've done my best to duplicate her delicious results—it comes delightfully close!

½ TSP KOSHER SALT

2 LARGE HEADS BROCCOLI, BROKEN INTO FLORETS, STEM PEELED AND THINLY SLICED

1 TBSP RICE VINEGAR

1 TBSP SOY SAUCE

1 TBSP MIRIN

1 TBSP TOASTED SESAME OIL

½ TSP SRIRACHA SAUCE

2 TBSP ORGANIC REFINED OLIVE OIL (SEE OLIVE OIL, PAGE 18)

1 TBSP BLACK SESAME SEEDS, TOASTED (SUBSTITUTE WHITE SESAME SEEDS)

FLAKY SALT FOR FINISHING

Bring a large pot of water to boil over high heat. Add the salt and then the broccoli to the pot and cook for 4 to 6 minutes, or until just tender. Drain the water and then run cold water over the broccoli until cool.

In the bottom of a serving bowl, whisk together the vinegar, soy sauce, mirin, sesame oil, and Sriracha.

Heat the olive oil in a sauté pan over medium-low heat, add the broccoli, and sauté until just warm, stirring often. Transfer to the serving bowl, and toss with the sauce and sesame seeds. Taste, and serve with a pinch of flaky salt.

— DRIED SHRIMP RICE —

Dried shrimp paste, which goes by a dozen different names, from Vietnam to Indonesia, southern China to Laos, is potent stuff. Add a little to this and that as you cook any kind of Asian food and the flavors explode. Go easy—it's salty.

1 CUP/200 G JASMINE RICE, RINSED AND DRAINED

2 CUPS/480 ML WATER

1 TBSP SHRIMP PASTE (WITH OR WITHOUT SOYBEAN OIL)

2 TBSP COCONUT FAT (SUBSTITUTE BUTTER)

6 GREEN ONIONS, TRIMMED TOP AND BOTTOM AND THINLY SLICED (USE IT ALL)

1 TBSP RICE WINE VINEGAR

FLAKY SALT (OPTIONAL)

Combine the rice, water, and shrimp paste in a medium saucepan. Cook, covered, over medium heat for 12 to 15 minutes, or until the rice is tender and the water has evaporated. Remove from the heat and use a fork to gently stir in the coconut fat, green onions, and vinegar. Taste, adding a pinch of flaky salt if the rice needs it. Serve warm or cold.

CHAR SIU STEAMED BUNS, CHARRED BRUSSELS SPROUTS WITH SLICED CHILES, AND BEAN SPROUT SALAD

SERVES 6 TO 8; MAKES 48 BUNS

Thanks to David Chang of Momofuku fame, these buns have become something of a cult item. With their plush exterior and salty-sweet filling, it's not difficult to see why. Unlike many faddish foods, these mini-sandwiches are deserving of the fuss. Don't shy away from the endeavor with visions of gluey dough in a steamer pot; making your own is far simpler than it might seem at first glance. When they work—as they will—you'll have the definitive crowd-pleaser to deliver to the table. Fortunately, this recipe makes enough to feed a table full of enthusiasts.

— CHAR SIU STEAMED BUNS —

2 TSP INSTANT DRY YEAST

2 CUPS/480 ML WARM WATER (ABOUT 105°F/40°C)

1/2 CUP/50 G CONFECTIONERS' SUGAR

1 TBSP CORNSTARCH

2 TBSP ORGANIC CANOLA OIL

KOSHER SALT

2 TBSP RICE VINEGAR

5 CUPS/635 G ALL-PURPOSE FLOUR

1 TSP BAKING POWDER

1/4 CUP/60 ML SAMBAL OELEK

1/2 CUP/120 ML HOISIN SAUCE

1 RECIPE CHAR SIU (PAGE 171)

1 CUCUMBER, THINLY SLICED

1 CUP/40 G FRESH CILANTRO LEAVES

SRIRACHA SAUCE FOR SERVING

In the bowl of a stand mixer (or in a mixing bowl), combine the yeast and water. Observe for 1 minute to be sure the yeast is live; it should subtly bubble and foam. Whisk in the confectioners' sugar, cornstarch, canola oil, $\frac{1}{2}$ tsp salt, and the vinegar. Add the flour and baking powder and mix briefly with a wooden spoon. Set in the stand mixer with the dough hook attached and work on medium speed for 5 to 7 minutes, or until the dough is smooth, slightly sticky, but easy to handle and can be shaped into a ball. (If you're working by hand, mix thoroughly and turn out the dough onto your work surface. Knead, using as little extra flour as possible, for 10 to 15 minutes.) Use a little oil to coat your hands and form the dough into a tidy ball. Lightly coat a large bowl (or the bowl of the stand mixer) with oil and set the dough to rise in a warm spot for 30 to 40 minutes, or until doubled in size.

Cover two baking sheets with parchment paper, and then coat the parchment with oil. On a clean, lightly floured surface, flatten the dough with your hand without working it or changing its round shape. Use a pastry cutter or a knife to cut the circle of dough into eight wedges, as you would a pizza. Work with one wedge at a time, and keep the rest covered with a clean towel. Roll a wedge into a short log (about 6 in/15 cm long), and then cut the log into six pieces (a little less than 1 oz/30 g each). Use a rolling pin to flatten each piece into a circle roughly 5 in/12 cm across. Place each circle facedown on the baking sheet, gently moving it around for a minute to coat one side with oil. Fold the oiled surface in on itself to form a half-moon. Place the raw buns in straight rows on the prepared baking sheet, close together but not touching, and cover them with a clean towel. Repeat with the remaining dough.

Using your sharpest paring knife, cut the parchment paper to make little individual squares under each bun. Set the raw buns aside to rise for 15 to 30 minutes. Set up a pot with a steamer basket or rack, add water, and bring to a boil. Cook the buns in batches by setting them, parchment and all, to steam for 3 minutes. They're done when the dough is set but not discolored—trust me, 3 minutes is just right. Remove the cooked buns to a large tray and begin making the sandwiches. Cook the remaining buns and set to cool if not using right away. (You may use them for a hungry crowd the same night or for leftovers the next day.)

In a small bowl, mix together the sambal oelek and hoisin. Gently open the buns and coat with a layer of sambal-hoisin mixture. Thinly slice the char siu, sprinkle with a pinch of salt, and cover the base of each bun with a single layer of meat. Place 2 or 3 cucumber slices on top of the meat, and finish with plenty of cilantro leaves. Gently press the top and bottom of the bun together. Serve the buns with Sriracha sauce on the side.

CHAR SIU
2½ TO 3 LB/1 TO 1.4 KG

3- TO 3½-LB/1.4- TO 1.6-KG BONE-IN SHOULDER ROAST, PRESLICED OR WHOLE (LOOK FOR SHOULDER PICNIC, BLADE ROAST, BOSTON PICNIC, BOSTON BUTT, OR PICNIC ROAST)

¼ CUP/60 ML HOISIN SAUCE

¼ CUP/60 ML SHAOXING COOKING WINE (SUBSTITUTE SERCIAL SHERRY)

2 TBSP DARK SOY SAUCE

2 TBSP LIGHT SOY SAUCE

2 TBSP OYSTER SAUCE

½ TSP CHINESE FIVE-SPICE POWDER

1 CUBE FERMENTED TOFU, PLUS 2 TBSP OF THE LIQUID (OPTIONAL)

2 TBSP HONEY

2 TBSP HOT WATER

If your meat is not already sliced, cut it into slices 1 to 1½ in/ 2.5 to 4 cm thick, working around and cutting away gristle and bone. (Keep the slices as large as you can without retaining the gristle.) Lay the meat on a cutting board and puncture all over on both sides with a fork.

In a large, flat baking dish (such as a glass casserole dish), whisk together the hoisin, cooking wine, dark soy sauce, light soy sauce, oyster sauce, five-spice powder, and fermented tofu cube and liquid (if using). Lay the meat in the dish, turning to thoroughly coat. Allow the meat to marinate for at least 1 hour on the counter, or for up to 24 hours in the refrigerator. (Allow the meat to rest for 30 minutes to 1 hour on the counter to take the chill off if refrigerated.)

Preheat the oven to 375°F/190°C. Line a rimmed baking sheet with parchment, and set a wire rack (such as a cookie rack) securely on top. Remove the meat from the marinade without scraping off the excess and lay it on the rack. It's best if the slices don't touch, but don't fuss too much. Mix together the honey and water in a small dish. Roast the meat for 10 minutes, remove it from the oven, and use a pastry brush to coat the surface with the honey mixture. Return the meat to the oven and roast for another 20 to 25 minutes, or until it feels fairly firm when poked and an instant-read thermometer inserted into the thickest part of a steak registers approximately 145°F/63°C. Reduce the oven temperature so it's as low as you can get it, cover the meat, and keep warm until you're ready to slice it. (Or you can refrigerate it for up to 3 days.)

— CHARRED BRUSSELS SPROUTS — WITH SLICED CHILES

I was inspired by a side special I shared with Bill LeBlond, longtime cookbook editor, one night at a deafeningly loud bistro in New York's East Village. The flavor of these terrific Brussels sprouts came through the din, even if not much else could.

2 LB/910 G BRUSSELS SPROUTS, TRIMMED AND HALVED

¼ CUP/60 ML ORGANIC HIGH-HEAT OIL (SEE HIGH-TEMPERATURE COOKING OILS, PAGE 17)

3 GARLIC CLOVES, MINCED

1 TSP KOSHER SALT

2 SERRANO CHILES, SLICED, WITH SEEDS

¼ CUP/30 G GRATED PECORINO ROMANO CHEESE

Preheat the broiler. In a large mixing bowl, toss together the Brussels sprouts, oil, garlic, salt, and chiles. Spread out the Brussels sprouts on a baking sheet (lined with parchment if you like) and broil for 8 to 10 minutes. They should be just tender at the center, with the exterior leaves alarmingly well browned—almost charred. Sprinkle the cheese on top and serve.

— BEAN SPROUT SALAD —

Banchan is the name for the ubiquitous side dishes that accompany most Korean meals. This one, based on bean sprouts, is a standard, which comes in many varieties. Here's mine.

8 OZ/225 G BEAN SPROUTS

1/4 CUP/30 G SESAME SEEDS, TOASTED

2 TBSP TOASTED SESAME OIL

1 GARLIC CLOVE, MINCED

2 TSP FISH SAUCE

1/4 CUP/10 G SNIPPED FRESH CHIVES

1/2 ENGLISH (SEEDLESS) CUCUMBER, CUT INTO 1-IN/2.5-CM DICE

1 TSP RICE VINEGAR

Bring a pot of water to a boil, submerge the bean sprouts, and cook for 3 to 4 minutes, until they lose their raw flavor. Drain and rinse under cold water until cool. Shake dry and transfer to a serving bowl. Toss with the sesame seeds, sesame oil, garlic, fish sauce, chives, cucumber, and vinegar. Serve cold.

BLACK SOY RIB-END ROAST
WITH ROASTED YAMS AND MAITAKE MUSHROOMS

SERVES 4

A roast marinated in soy (particularly black mushroom soy) is rich, dark, and salty. It makes a gorgeous plate when sliced and paired with the bright orange yams and the flowery white elegance of maitake mushrooms. Make a big pot of fragrant jasmine rice to round out the plate. A few of those good Mixed Pickles (page 210) would not go amiss if you happen to have some kicking around in the refrigerator.

— BLACK SOY RIB-END ROAST —

2 TBSP DARK MUSHROOM SOY OR TAMARI SAUCE

1 TBSP ORGANIC HIGH-HEAT OIL (SEE HIGH-TEMPERATURE COOKING OILS, PAGE 17)

1 TBSP DRY MUSTARD

1 TBSP HONEY

ONE 1½- TO 2-LB/680- TO 910-G RIB-END ROAST

1 RECIPE JASMINE RICE (PAGE 185) FOR SERVING

1 RECIPE ROASTED YAMS AND MAITAKE MUSHROOMS (RECIPE FOLLOWS)

FLAKY OR COARSE SALT FOR FINISHING

1 LIME, QUARTERED

¼ CUP/10 G COARSELY CHOPPED FRESH CILANTRO

Combine the soy sauce, oil, dry mustard, and honey in the bottom of a large mixing bowl. Put the roast in the bowl and coat all over with the mixture. Marinate, if you have time, for up to 1 hour on the kitchen counter, or for 24 hours in the refrigerator.

When you're ready to cook, preheat the oven to 400°F/200°C. (Bring the meat to room temperature if it isn't already.) Place the meat, wet with the marinade, in a large cast-iron frying pan or in a small roasting pan. Roast for 20 minutes, reduce the heat to 300°F/150°C, and cook for another 25 to 35 minutes, or until the meat reaches 145°F/63°C on an instant-read thermometer inserted in the center. Remove from the oven and allow the meat to rest in the hot pan for 5 minutes before carving.

I like to make the plate with a generous pile of jasmine rice, a stack of roasted yams and maitake mushrooms right up next to it, and some of that delicious pork laid over the two. Serve each plate with a sprinkle of flaky salt, a squeeze of lime juice, and a sprinkle of the cilantro.

— ROASTED YAMS AND MAITAKE MUSHROOMS —

Yams and mushrooms are the most earthy, delicious combination. If you can't find maitakes, use shiitakes instead.

2 LB/910 G YAMS

1 TBSP MUSTARD SEED

1 TBSP ORGANIC HIGH-HEAT OIL (SEE HIGH-TEMPERATURE COOKING OILS, PAGE 17)

1 1/2 TSP KOSHER SALT

2 TBSP BUTTER

1 LB/455 G MAITAKE MUSHROOMS, TRIMMED INTO LARGE BITE-SIZE PIECES

COARSE OR FLAKY SALT FOR FINISHING

Preheat the oven to 300°F/150°C. Peel the yams until all the exposed flesh is bright orange. Cut into 1-in-/2.5-cm-thick rounds, and then quarter to make bite-size chunks. Put the chunks in a mixing bowl and toss with the mustard seed, oil, and 1 tsp of the kosher salt.

Spread out the yams on a baking sheet (lined with parchment if you like). Cook for 40 to 60 minutes, or until soft. To finish, turn up the oven to 400°F/200°C for 10 minutes to brown. When you take the pork out to rest it before carving, turn up the heat and finish the yams.

Heat a large frying pan set over high heat. Add the butter, swirl, and add the mushrooms and the remaining 1/2 tsp kosher salt. Cook the mushrooms hot and fast, stirring frequently, for 3 to 5 minutes, or until the raw taste is gone and a few edges are browned.

Toss the mushrooms and yams together in a large serving bowl, add a pinch of coarse salt, and serve.

PORK DUMPLINGS IN RICH STOCK

WITH CUCUMBER–ASIAN PEAR SALAD

SERVES 4 TO 6; MAKES 40 TO 50 DUMPLINGS

Resisting pork dumplings doesn't come easily to me. This recipe
makes plenty; serve them simply, the better to keep the focus on
the porky little packets themselves. Feel free to cook them all up,
half in a steamer and half in the stock. Or, set the extra aside
in the freezer for another day. One final note: Have no fear; it's
not at all difficult to make dumplings.

— PORK DUMPLINGS IN RICH STOCK —

2 TBSP ORGANIC HIGH-HEAT OIL (SEE HIGH-TEMPERATURE COOKING OILS, PAGE 17)

5 SHIITAKE MUSHROOMS, STEMMED AND MINCED

KOSHER SALT

1 LB/455 G GROUND PORK

¾ CUP/65 G SLICED GREEN ONIONS

1 TBSP SHRIMP PASTE (WITH OR WITHOUT SOYBEAN OIL)

1 TBSP DARK SOY SAUCE

1 CUP/90 G FINELY CHOPPED NAPA OR SAVOY CABBAGE

¼ TSP CAYENNE PEPPER

3 GARLIC CLOVES, MINCED

½ TSP BAKING SODA

40 TO 50 DUMPLING WRAPPERS (WONTON OR EVEN POT STICKER WRAPPERS WILL WORK)

1 RECIPE RICH STOCK (PAGE 181)

4 OZ/115 G MIXED ASIAN BABY GREENS, SUCH AS TATSOI, BOK CHOY, BROCCOLI RABE, MIZUNA, AND SPINACH, AMONG OTHERS

¼ CUP/10 G SNIPPED FRESH CHIVES

⇒

Heat the oil in a medium sauté pan set over medium heat and add the mushrooms and ¼ tsp kosher salt. Cook for 6 to 8 minutes, or until fragrant and soft. Put the cooked mushrooms in a large mixing bowl and add 1 tsp salt, the ground pork, green onions, shrimp paste, soy sauce, cabbage, cayenne, garlic, and baking soda. Refrigerate the dumpling mixture until you're ready to stuff the dumplings.

Lay out five dumpling wrappers on your work surface. Set a small dish of water next to your dumpling bowl. Dip your fingers in the water, dotting the moisture all around the rim of each wrapper. Next, place about 2 tsp filling in a neat pile in the center of each wrapper. If your wrappers are round, bring the two opposite sides together to form a half-moon, pinching carefully around where the edges meet, until each dumpling is tightly sealed. Place the finished dumplings on a baking sheet lined with parchment (or lightly dusted with flour). Repeat until you have used all the wrappers or all the filling. (You can freeze any remaining filling, if you're inclined. You can also freeze the extra dumplings. Lay them flat on a baking sheet in the freezer, and once frozen, bag them up.)

Bring the Rich Stock to a boil in a large saucepan set over high heat. Add twenty-one dumplings and cook for 5 to 7 minutes, or until the dumplings are tender, not doughy, and very hot throughout. Test one by cutting it open. Taste the stock and add a little salt, as needed. Set out four large, deep soup bowls, and distribute the greens and dumplings before ladling on the hot broth. Sprinkle with chives and serve.

— CUCUMBER-ASIAN PEAR SALAD —

This is an antidote to the strong, spicy main course. It's an unexpectedly agreeable combination, which takes minutes to toss together.

1 ASIAN PEAR, SKIN ON, CHILLED AND COARSELY CHOPPED INTO 1-IN/2.5-CM CHUNKS

1 LARGE CUCUMBER, CHILLED, PEELED, COARSELY CHOPPED INTO 1-IN/2.5-CM CHUNKS

1 TSP CHINKIANG VINEGAR (SUBSTITUTE PLAIN RICE VINEGAR)

1 TSP BLACK SESAME SEEDS

PINCH OF KOSHER SALT

Toss the Asian pear, cucumber, vinegar, sesame seeds, and salt together in a serving bowl and serve right away.

PORK BELLY RAMEN NOODLE BOWL

SERVES 4

There's nothing quite like working your way through a big bowl of this Rich Stock, pushed to its most flavorful limits with seaweed and shaved bonito flakes and then combined with springy noodles, fatty belly, and a runny egg yolk. The radishes, carrots, cilantro, and seaweed add dimensions of flavor and texture to what is, I think, one of the most irresistible single-bowl eating experiences I know. I recognize that's a lot to live up to—but I'm confident you'll agree. If you think this isn't enough dinner, you can make a spectacular feast by adding a batch of Char Siu Steamed Buns (page 169) to eat on the side.

Here, you'll find the easiest, most fail-safe method for slow cooking pork belly, but it does require a little planning. It will give you twice the amount of belly you'll need, but there's nothing quite like having a piece of this goodness in your refrigerator, cooked and ready to crisp for any number of indulgent applications.

— PORK BELLY RAMEN NOODLE BOWL —

FIVE-SPICE PORK BELLY

1 TO 2 LB/455 TO 910 G PORK BELLY

¼ CUP/60 ML DARK SOY SAUCE

2 TSP CHINESE FIVE-SPICE POWDER

7 OZ/200 G CURLY JAPANESE NOODLES (RAMEN), COOKED ACCORDING TO THE PACKAGE DIRECTIONS AND RINSED IN COLD WATER

1 TSP TOASTED SESAME OIL

1 CUP/70 G THINLY SLICED RED CABBAGE

1 TBSP ORGANIC CANOLA OIL

1 LB/455 G SHIITAKE MUSHROOMS, STEMMED AND THINLY SLICED

¼ TSP KOSHER SALT

1 LARGE OR 2 SMALL CHERRY BELLE RADISHES, THINLY SLICED (ANY VARIETY WILL DO)

4 EGGS, BOILED FOR 6 MINUTES

1 RECIPE RICH STOCK (PAGE 181)

2 CARROTS, PEELED AND JULIENNED (CUT INTO MATCHSTICKS)

¼ CUP/8 G FUERU WAKAME (DRIED SEAWEED)

¼ CUP/10 G FRESH CILANTRO LEAVES

FLAKY SALT FOR FINISHING

SRIRACHA HOT SAUCE FOR SERVING

To make the pork belly: Preheat the oven to 200°F/95°C. Place the pork belly in a large mixing bowl with the soy sauce and five-spice powder and turn to thoroughly coat. Place the pork belly, skin-side up, in a large cast-iron frying pan or a small roasting pan and place it in the oven. Cook for 3 to 5 hours, depending on the thickness of the meat. It will not burn at such a moderate oven temperature—it will simply render more fat. It should be falling-apart tender and the fat should be supple. Slice the pork belly, leaving the layer of fat intact, into eight 1-in-/2.5-cm-thick slices. Set aside. Reheat the meat before serving, as needed, by laying the sliced belly on a baking sheet and returning it to the oven at the same low temperature.

Toss the noodles with the sesame oil in a large mixing bowl and portion them out in the bottom of four large soup bowls. (Deep bowls are best, but pasta plates will work, too.) Place the cabbage over the noodles, and make a little nest on top of each serving.

Heat the canola oil in a medium sauté pan set over medium-high heat, add the mushrooms and kosher salt, and cook for 5 to 8 minutes, or until soft and fragrant. Tuck a portion of the mushrooms on one side of each bowl in a clump and the radish slices opposite. Place the sliced belly on the remaining sides of the bowl, one on each side, opposite one another. Drain the eggs, rinsing them briefly with cold water so you can handle them. Using a knife and a teaspoon, whack the top off each egg, and then carefully scoop out the egg, taking care not to break the yolk, and place it on top of the cabbage.

Bring the stock to a boil in a medium saucepan over high heat. Add the carrots and wakame, cover, and boil for 1 minute. Pour the boiling stock into the bowls, dividing it evenly. Sprinkle with the cilantro and a tiny pinch of flaky salt, and serve. Put a bottle of Sriracha on the table, in case anyone likes a little heat with their ramen, as I most definitely do.

RICH STOCK
4 CUPS/960 ML

2 1/2 LB/1.2 KG BONY CHICKEN PARTS
(WHOLE RAW CARCASS, LEGS, THIGHS, FEET)

1 1/2 LB/680 G BONY PORK PARTS
(HOCK, FEET, NECK BONES, SHANK)

1 LB/455 G SHIITAKE MUSHROOMS, STEMS ONLY
(RESERVE CAPS FOR THE SOUP)

3 TO 5 CARROTS, SNAPPED INTO THIRDS

ONE 3-IN/7.5-CM PIECE FRESH GINGER, PEELED

1/2 ONION, QUARTERED

1 TSP CORIANDER SEED

1/4 CUP/8 G FUERU WAKAME (DRIED SEAWEED)

HEAPING 2 TBSP SHAVED BONITO FLAKES

3 QT/2.8 L COLD WATER

In a large stockpot, combine the chicken parts, pork parts, shiitake stems, carrots, ginger, onion, coriander seed, wakame, and bonito flakes. Cover with the water and bring to a boil over high heat. Turn down the heat as soon as the liquid boils, and begin skimming the surface to remove any scum. Continue to skim and simmer, uncovered, over medium-low heat for 2 hours. Strain the stock into a large saucepan and set aside until ready to use. It will keep, refrigerated, for 3 days, or, frozen, for up to 3 months.

BELLY-TOFU STIR-FRY
WITH JASMINE RICE

SERVES 4

A stir-fry can be a greasy, sodden mess in the wrong hands. In the right ones, it showcases a mix of fresh vegetables, the contrasting tastes and textures surpassing expectations. This stir-fry falls into the latter category—the only fatty thing about it is the pork belly, and that's the kind of fat that's worth the sacrifice of a little expendable dietary virtue. Besides, its sins of gluttony are definitely canceled out by the hypervirtuous vegetables. Be sure to work hot and fast over the most powerful burner you have.

— BELLY-TOFU STIR-FRY —

2 TBSP CORNSTARCH

2 TBSP SOY SAUCE

1 TBSP FISH SAUCE

1 TSP VEGETABLE OIL, PLUS 1 TBSP

8 OZ/225 G SLOW-COOKED PORK BELLY
(PAGE 67), CUBED

KOSHER SALT

8 OZ/225 G SHIITAKE MUSHROOMS,
STEMMED AND SLICED

1 STALK LEMONGRASS, CUT INTO THIN ROUNDS
(TENDER PART ONLY)

1 SMALL FINGER FRESH GINGER, PEELED AND
COARSELY CHOPPED

6 OZ/170 G FIRM TOFU, CUBED

1 TSP CORIANDER SEED

1 TSP DRY MUSTARD

$\frac{1}{2}$ TSP GROUND TURMERIC

$\frac{1}{4}$ RED ONION, COARSELY CHOPPED

1 LARGE HEAD BROCCOLI, CUT INTO
BITE-SIZE FLORETS

$\frac{1}{2}$ ORANGE OR RED BELL PEPPER, THINLY SLICED

1 SERRANO OR THAI CHILE, THINLY SLICED, PLUS
MORE FOR SERVING (OPTIONAL)

4 OZ/115 G SUGAR SNAP PEAS, TRIMMED

2 OZ/55G BEAN SPROUTS

$\frac{1}{4}$ CUP/10 G CHOPPED FRESH THAI BASIL
(SUBSTITUTE MINT OR A MIX OF MINT
AND ITALIAN BASIL)

$\frac{1}{4}$ CUP/35 G CHOPPED ROASTED SALTED PEANUTS

JASMINE RICE (PAGE 185)

SRIRACHA SAUCE FOR SERVING (OPTIONAL)

Preheat the oven to 180°F/80 C. In a small bowl, make a slurry of the cornstarch, soy sauce, and fish sauce. Set aside.

Heat a wok or large cast-iron frying pan over high heat until it smokes. Add the 1 tsp vegetable oil, swirl to heat, and add the pork belly. Cook, frequently moving the meat up the sides of the wok, for 2 to 3 minutes, or until fragrant, very hot, and beginning to brown. Transfer to a plate, leaving the fat behind. Sprinkle the pork with a pinch of salt and keep warm in the oven.

Add the mushrooms, lemongrass, and ginger to the wok and cook for 2 to 3 minutes, moving and spreading them up the sides of the wok. The mushrooms are cooked when they've lost some volume and become fragrant. Transfer to a bowl and set aside. Add the remaining 1 tbsp oil to the wok, swirl to heat, and add the tofu, coriander seed, dry mustard, turmeric, and onion. Cook for 1 to 2 minutes, working the tofu up the sides of the wok. Don't worry if you break the tofu cubes—they're not meant to stay intact. When the spices are fragrant, add the broccoli, bell pepper, chile, and snap peas. Cook for 3 to 4 minutes, working it as you have the other ingredients, until the broccoli is almost cooked—a bit crunchier than you like it. Return the mushrooms to the wok and add the cornstarch slurry, along with the bean sprouts, Thai basil, and peanuts. Cook for 1 to 2 minutes, heating all the ingredients through. When the broccoli is tender, portion out the rice and then the tofu and vegetables on top. Scatter the reserved pork belly over the vegetables. Serve with Sriracha sauce or sliced chiles, if desired.

— JASMINE RICE —

This is a little like my Buttery Toast (page 68)—it's hardly a recipe at all. You're making rice! But in truth, getting it right is harder than it sounds much of the time. To begin with, rice should be rinsed and drained to remove some of the starch. The tricky part is figuring out the precise water-to-rice ratio because these numbers vary, depending on how fresh the rice is, how it's been stored, and the variety you're cooking. A rice cooker is a smart addition to any kitchen, eliminating the potential for scorching that makes timing so tricky. (I've "smoked" my rice by forgetting about it; I suspect most people have.) Try to get used to your particular brand of rice and hone the ratio of water to rice over time—and buy yourself a rice cooker! Zojirushi, made in Japan, is my pick.

1½ CUPS/285 G JASMINE RICE,
RINSED AND DRAINED

3 CUPS/720 ML WATER

Combine the rice and water in a medium saucepan with a tight-fitting lid. Set over medium heat and cook, covered, for 12 to 15 minutes, or until the water has evaporated and the rice is tender. Let the rice stand for a moment off the heat, fluff with a fork, and serve.

GLAZED DASHI MISO CHOPS
AND SOBA NOODLES WITH
ROASTED ASPARAGUS

SERVES 4

Bonito flakes, often used to make dashi, a rich stock, are
the magic Japanese way of infusing foods with umami—the
savory, almost meaty, fifth flavor (we already had sweet, sour,
salty, bitter), which has spread through the Western food
vocabulary in the last twenty years or so. Here the dashi is
already in the miso paste. Diluted to make a marinade and
then added to the glaze, it works magic on a chop.

— GLAZED DASHI MISO CHOPS —

4 TBSP/50 G DASHI MISO PASTE (YOU'LL FIND THIS
IN AN ASIAN SUPERMARKET, OR MAKE YOUR OWN
BY COMBINING 2 TBSP BONITO FLAKES WITH EQUAL
PARTS WATER AND WHITE MISO PASTE)

4 TBSP/60 ML WATER

FOUR 12-OZ TO 1-LB/340- TO 455-G THICK-CUT
BONE-IN CHOPS, 1 1/2 TO 2 IN/4 TO 5 CM THICK

1 TSP ORGANIC HIGH-HEAT OIL, PLUS 1 TBSP (SEE
HIGH-TEMPERATURE COOKING OILS, PAGE 17)

Mix together 2 tbsp of the miso paste and 2 tbsp of the water in
the bottom of a mixing bowl or glass baking dish. Lay the chops
in the marinade, turning and rubbing to coat thoroughly. Marinate for 1 hour on the counter, or, better yet, overnight in the
refrigerator. (Rest at room temperature for 30 minutes to 1 hour
to take the chill off before cooking if you do marinate in the
refrigerator.)

Preheat the oven to 300°F/150°C. Blot the excess moisture from the
chops and rub with the 1 tsp oil. Heat a large cast-iron pan over
high heat, add the remaining 1 tbsp oil, and, when it shimmers,
carefully place the chops in the pan. Brown the chops on each side
until they're the color of a walnut shell, 4 to 6 minutes per side.
To finish cooking, place them, pan and all, in the oven for 5 to

10 minutes, or until an instant-read thermometer inserted into the center of the fattest chop reads 140°F/60°C. (It will gain several degrees as it rests.) The meat is done when it's pink, but not bloody, and the texture is slightly granular, not slippery and smooth as it is when raw.

Turn off the oven, transfer the chops to a plate, and return them to the oven with the oven door slightly ajar, to keep them warm. Place the pan with all its grease and brown bits over medium heat and add the remaining 2 tbsp miso paste. Add any juice from the pan the chops are sitting in and stir, scraping the bottom of the pan. When it's hot, pour the glaze over the chops and serve.

— SOBA NOODLES WITH ROASTED ASPARAGUS —

Asparagus season is short, but I refuse to buy them from the Southern Hemisphere in winter. If you've missed out, make this recipe with green beans or sugar snap peas. Simply slice them lengthwise into halves or thirds. Really, any vegetable delicious raw but tasty when lightly cooked will work beautifully. Shaved carrots or beets would be ideal. The earthy notes of soba noodles would also be pleasing with the thoroughly cooked sweet richness of Roasted Yams and Maitake Mushrooms (page 175).

24 ASPARAGUS SPEARS (ABOUT 2 SMALL BUNCHES)

ONE 6-OZ/170-G PACKAGE SOBA (BUCKWHEAT NOODLES)

2 TBSP TOASTED SESAME OIL

1 TBSP FRESH LEMON JUICE, PLUS MORE IF NEEDED

2 TSP SAMBAL OELEK, PLUS MORE IF NEEDED

KOSHER SALT

Trim away the rough base of the asparagus and then cut off the flower (the tip). Shave the stalks and tough bottoms with a vegetable peeler (the bottoms will be tender when thinly shaved). Cut the tips into quarters or halves, depending on the size of the asparagus.

Cook the noodles in a large pot of boiling water according to the package directions. When the noodles are just tender but still al dente, add the asparagus to the pot, submerge the threads, and drain immediately. Rinse with cold water until cool and then drain thoroughly again. Shake the noodles or give them plenty of time to drip dry, as any residual liquid will water down the dressing. Put the noodles in a big serving bowl and toss with the sesame oil, lemon juice, sambal oelek, and ¾ tsp salt. Taste, adding additional salt, sambal, or lemon juice as you like.

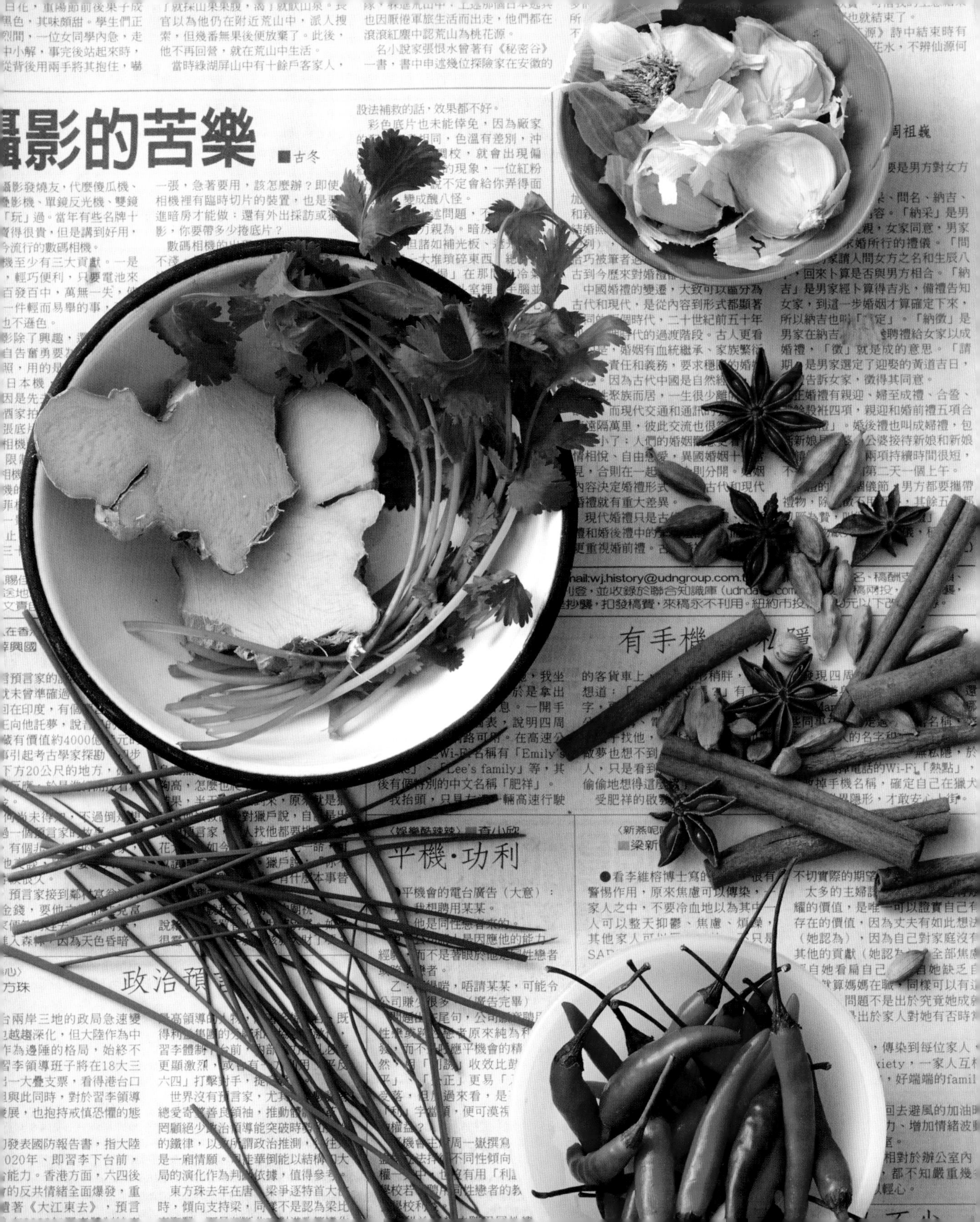
影的苦樂
古冬
有手機
平機·功利

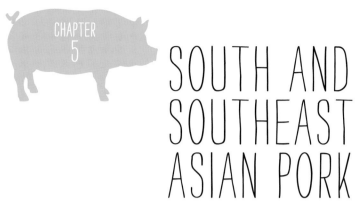

CHAPTER
5

SOUTH AND SOUTHEAST ASIAN PORK

SOUTH AND SOUTHEAST ASIAN PORK

This is an ambitious, far-reaching chapter that encompasses the traditions of a huge geographic area—Malaysia to India. Have a little fun: Do a big shop in an Asian supermarket when you can, or shop online (I like Asiansupermarket365.com); and don't stress if you don't have every single item listed in the recipe. For ingredients and shopping I'll repeat most of the litany from the Chinese and Japanese chapter. Lemongrass is also present here in ways it's not in the Chinese or Japanese recipes. Of the slightly more exotic items, you might want Shaoxing cooking wine and Chinkiang cooking wine; also chile paste (Chaotian Chili King is my favorite), chile bean paste (look for the same brand), shrimp paste, chile shrimp paste, dried shrimp, rice vinegar, hoisin sauce, toasted sesame oil, and pickled ginger. Of course, you can buy only what you need for a single recipe rather than buying every ingredient listed here.

DRINKS

Favorites include cold and hot green tea, beer, and, dread of dread, kombucha, which I adore but many people can't stand. Decide for yourself. I adore lighter beers with spicy food. I usually reach for a clean wheat beer, which won't interfere with my palate but will provide a refreshing antidote to spice and salt. I don't drink much wine with this kind of food. If you do, stick to dry Riesling or Sauvignon Blanc.

ON THE TABLE

This food, like Latin and Chinese, calls for lots of small plates
and bowls to share, including pickles, chiles, green onions, and
various fermented items, such as kimchi and tofu (it comes in jars).
Chopsticks are very much optional, as they're not traditional in
most cuisines represented here, but as I've said, I like them because
they slow me down, forcing me to focus on each bite.

SWEETS

Fruit is an ideal dessert when it follows spicy, salty food. Watermelon, mango, or pineapple are easy. And then there are lychees,
which I don't much like unless I'm really focused on eating them.
For more involved options, rice pudding made with unsweetened
coconut milk is easy and tasty. In summer, the most obvious choice
is tropical ices paired with a crispy, slightly salty cookie.

ONE-POT BRAISED COCONUT-MILK PORK

SERVES 4

This one-pot dinner entices not through its aggressive spices, unctuousness, or jarring flavors but through its mellow, unassuming goodness. My kind of comfort food comes in this precise form—the familiar scent of coconut milk and coriander mixed with bits of rich pork and plenty of vegetables. Versatile and fast, you can easily have this meal on the table in 30 minutes or less, if you take your time with your peeler to get all the vegetables into those long, fine strips. They cook quickly and come out irresistibly silky when prepared this way. A pot of fragrant jasmine rice is all you need to line the bottom of your bowl.

ONE 2-IN/5-CM PIECE FRESH GINGER, PEELED

3 CARROTS, PEELED

1 ORANGE OR RED SWEET PEPPER, SEEDED

1 EGGPLANT, SKIN ON

KOSHER SALT

1 TO 2 TBSP ORGANIC HIGH-HEAT OIL (SEE HIGH-TEMPERATURE COOKING OILS, PAGE 17) OR COCONUT FAT

1 LB/455 G PORK, FINELY CHOPPED (I USE BONE-IN SHOULDER OR LOIN CHOPS, BUT ANY CUT WILL DO)

3 OZ/85 G ENOKI MUSHROOMS, BASE TRIMMED (SUBSTITUTE THINLY SLICED SHIITAKE CAPS)

2 TSP CORIANDER SEED, CRUSHED

1/2 TSP GROUND TURMERIC

2 TBSP FISH SAUCE

TWO 13 1/2-OZ/405-ML CANS FULL-FAT COCONUT MILK

2 CUPS/480 ML WATER

1 CUP/55 G TIGHTLY PACKED FRESH SPINACH LEAVES, CUT INTO RIBBONS

1/4 CUP/10 G CHOPPED FRESH THAI BASIL (SUBSTITUTE ITALIAN BASIL, MINT, OR A COMBINATION)

1 RECIPE JASMINE RICE (PAGE 185)

Use a vegetable peeler to make about twelve thin strips out of the ginger, carrots, and sweet pepper. Set aside. Do the same with the eggplant after removing the center with the seeds. Put the eggplant strips in a bowl with a good pinch of salt and set aside.

Heat 1 tbsp of the oil in a large Dutch oven set over high heat. Add half the pork and cook until lightly browned, 5 to 8 minutes. Transfer to a plate and brown the remaining pork. When it's done, return the first batch of browned meat to the pot and add the mushrooms, coriander seed, turmeric, and fish sauce. Add more oil if the pan is dry, turn the heat to medium, and cook for 1 to 2 minutes, stirring constantly. Stir in the ginger, carrots, sweet pepper, eggplant, coconut milk, and water. When the liquid boils, turn the heat to low and simmer for 12 to 15 minutes, or until the eggplant is silky and delicious. Add the spinach and half the Thai basil, stir thoroughly, and serve over the rice with the remaining Thai basil scattered on top.

MEATBALL BANH MI
WITH CARROT-DAIKON PICKLES AND CARROT-SESAME SLAW

SERVES 4

Tofu, sausage, egg, liver, sardines, beef, chicken, pork, and meatballs—yes, meatballs. They all fall under the expansive banh mi umbrella. In this case, I've stuck with meatballs made with ground pork, a few chicken livers for depth of flavor, a pinch of five-spice powder, coriander seed, and plenty of fish sauce for that super-umami high note. If you aren't already on the trendy banh mi boat party, this is your chance. Look for a soft, thin baguette— not the usual chewy, crusty ones you might seek out if you were looking for a proper French loaf. Once you've added pickled daikon, carrots, cilantro, and a few little sauces, you've got a memorable sandwich. Believe me, there are plenty of good reasons to go wild for this highly versatile Franco-Vietnamese vestige of colonialism.

— MEATBALL BANH MI —

1 TBSP BUTTER

2 CHICKEN LIVERS (PREFERABLY ORGANIC)

1 LB/455 G GROUND PORK

1 TSP CORIANDER SEED, LIGHTLY CRUSHED

2 TBSP FISH SAUCE

2 TSP BROWN SUGAR (DARK OR LIGHT)

1/2 TSP BAKING POWDER

1/2 TSP CHINESE FIVE-SPICE POWDER

1/2 TSP KOSHER SALT

BLACK PEPPER

2 TBSP *MAE PLOY* (SWEET CHILE SAUCE)

1/4 CUP/60 ML MAYONNAISE

1/4 CUP/60 ML SAMBAL OELEK

1 OR 2 BAGUETTES, CUT IN HALF LENGTHWISE, AND THEN INTO 4- TO 6-IN/10- TO 15-CM LENGTHS

1 JALAPEÑO OR SERRANO CHILE, THINLY SLICED

1/2 ENGLISH (SEEDLESS) CUCUMBER, THINLY SLICED

1 RECIPE CARROT-DAIKON PICKLES (RECIPE FOLLOWS)

1 TBSP SOY SAUCE

1 LARGE BUNCH CILANTRO, LEAVES ONLY

Preheat the oven to 350°F/180°C. Lightly oil a baking sheet. Melt the butter in a small saucepan set over medium-high heat, add the chicken livers, and sauté, shaking the pan frequently to prevent sticking, for 2 to 3 minutes on each side. Set the livers on a cutting board to cool briefly before coarsely chopping. Place the livers in a large bowl with the ground pork, coriander seed, fish sauce, brown sugar, baking powder, five-spice powder, salt, and a few grinds of black pepper. Mix well and form the meat into balls slightly smaller than a golf ball. Set them on the prepared baking sheet (or on a baking sheet covered with a sheet of parchment instead). You should have twelve to fifteen meatballs total. Bake for 20 to 25 minutes, or until very hot and no longer pink in the center.

In a small bowl mix together the *mae ploy*, mayonnaise, and sambal oelek. Spread a thin layer of the mixture on the cut side of each of the bottom slices of the baguette, and lay on a few chile slices, cucumber slices, a generous dose of Carrot-Daikon Pickles, and three or four meatballs. Give the meatballs a drizzle of soy sauce and finish with a generous layer of cilantro leaves before attempting to close it up. Be sure to have extra napkins at hand—preferably those you don't mind making a mess of—when serving.

— CARROT-DAIKON PICKLES —

Andrea Nguyen, the goddess of Vietnamese cooking, explains that these pickles are called *do chua*, and they're a staple of Vietnamese kitchens, as they add a tart, crisp note to just about anything. Make a big jar and spread them around.

½ LARGE DAIKON, PEELED AND JULIENNED (CUT INTO MATCHSTICKS)

3 CARROTS, PEELED AND JULIENNED

½ TSP KOSHER SALT

1 TBSP SUGAR

1½ CUPS/360 ML RICE VINEGAR

1½ CUPS/360 ML WATER

Place the daikon and carrots in a 1-qt/960-ml glass canning jar. Add the salt, sugar, vinegar, and water. The vegetables should be covered with liquid. (Add a little more vinegar and water in equal parts if they're not.) Screw the lid down tightly, shake, and refrigerate for 30 minutes before using. You want them crispy and chilly for high contrast on your sandwich. They will keep, refrigerated, for 3 to 4 weeks.

— CARROT-SESAME SLAW —

Buy firm (not bendable) carrots, with their frilly green tops
still on, removing them as soon as you get home. The beet and
mint give this slaw a vibrant flavor and contrast nicely
with the carrots.

6 TO 8 CARROTS, PEELED AND SHREDDED

1 SMALL RED BEET, PEELED AND SHREDDED

GRATED ZEST OF 1 LIME

2 TBSP RICE VINEGAR

2 TBSP ORGANIC REFINED OLIVE OIL
(SEE OLIVE OILS, PAGE 18)

1/2 TSP SUGAR

1/2 TSP KOSHER SALT

1/2 CUP/20 G COARSELY CHOPPED FRESH MINT OR
THAI BASIL

1/4 CUP/30 G SESAME SEEDS, TOASTED

Combine the carrots, beet, lime zest, rice vinegar, olive oil, sugar,
salt, mint, and sesame seeds in a large serving bowl. Toss well
and serve.

PULLED PORK SANDWICHES
WITH SICHUAN PEPPER SAUCE, SAMBAL MAYONNAISE, AND PICKLED ONIONS

SERVES 4

This is a long cooking endeavor that makes a quantity of pulled pork. Cook it for a party or plan on eating the pulled pork in cross-cultural tacos and sandwiches for the next few days. The pork will definitely benefit from marinating overnight. The big flavor of the meat and its potent sauce would go with a big pot of plain Jasmine Rice (page 185), and it would be complemented by Peanut-Coconut Slaw.

— PULLED PORK SANDWICHES —

ONE 6- TO 8-LB/2.7- TO 3.6-KG BONE-IN SHOULDER ROAST (LOOK FOR SHOULDER PICNIC, BLADE ROAST, BOSTON PICNIC, BOSTON BUTT, OR PICNIC ROAST)

2 TBSP SAMBAL OELEK

2 TBSP RICE VINEGAR

2 TBSP THAI FISH SAUCE

2 TBSP SHAOXING COOKING WINE

2 TBSP ROASTED CHILE PASTE

2 TBSP DARK SOY SAUCE

2 TBSP DRY MUSTARD

1 TBSP RAW SUGAR

¾ TO 1 CUP/180 TO 240 ML SICHUAN PEPPER SAUCE (PAGE 200)

8 SLICES SOURDOUGH BREAD, TOASTED; OR 2 LONG, CRISP BAGUETTES, SPLIT; OR 8 SMALL SOFT BUNS

SAMBAL MAYONNAISE (PAGE 200)

½ CUCUMBER, PEELED AND VERY THINLY SLICED

PICKLED ONIONS (PAGE 201)

1 BUNCH FRESH CILANTRO, LEAVES ONLY

PEANUT-COCONUT SLAW (PAGE 211) FOR SERVING

Preheat the oven to 200°F/95°C. Make small slits all over the roast, cutting into the layer of fat on top and into the fleshy parts. In a large mixing bowl, combine the sambal oelek, rice vinegar, fish sauce, cooking wine, chile paste, soy sauce, mustard, and sugar. Stir together and put the meat in the bowl, rubbing the marinade all over with your hands to be sure it gets into all the crevices. Let it sit out at room temperature to marinate for 30 minutes to 1 hour. (You may refrigerate the meat to marinate for up to 24 hours; just be sure to rest it at room temperature for 30 minutes to take the chill off before cooking.) Place the roast in a large cast-iron frying pan or a small roasting pan, put it in the oven, and cook for 5 to 6 hours, turning every hour or so. The meat is done when the exterior is crispy and the interior tears apart easily. It should register around 180°F/80°C at its center.

Let the roast cool, and then pull it with a fork or your hands, creating long threads of well-cooked meat. Don't cut it—or cut the crusty exterior only, if you must. Place the meat in a large mixing bowl and toss with the Sichuan pepper sauce. Taste as you season, adding additional sauce as needed. The longer it sits, the more sauce the pork will absorb, so check your seasoning again before assembling your sandwiches.

Coat the bread on both sides with plenty of sambal mayonnaise. Next, layer on the cucumber slices so that they cover the bread and just peek over the edges. Before adding the meat, lay on a generous bunch of pickled onions with a few bits of coriander seed clinging to them. Finally, give each sandwich a generous pile of meat and a handful of cilantro leaves. Close up the sandwiches and serve with the Peanut-Coconut Slaw. If you're going back for seconds (or thirds) the next day, wrap the meat tightly in foil and set in a 200°F/95°C oven for 15 to 20 minutes, or until it's hot.

— SICHUAN PEPPER SAUCE —

This is a delirious mash-up of Chinese cooking ingredients. You'll like the results—spicy, complex, and contrary. With this sauce, I suspect your pulled pork sandwich will be unlike any you've had before. A quick trip to an Asian grocery will supply you with everything you need if you don't already have it on hand.

½ CUP/120 ML SHAOXING COOKING WINE

¼ CUP/60 ML OYSTER SAUCE

1 TBSP SHRIMP PASTE (WITH OR WITHOUT SOYBEAN OIL)

3 TBSP DARK MUSHROOM SOY SAUCE (REGULAR SOY IS FINE, TOO)

3 GARLIC CLOVES, CRUSHED AND COARSELY CHOPPED

2 TBSP SICHUAN PEPPERCORNS, CRUSHED

¼ CUP/25 G CHOPPED GINGER

3 WHOLE STAR ANISE

1 TBSP CHILE PASTE

1 TBSP FERMENTED BLACK BEANS, MASHED

1 TBSP DRY MUSTARD

1 TBSP PEANUT OR VEGETABLE OIL

¼ CUP/60 ML CHINKIANG VINEGAR (SUBSTITUTE REGULAR RICE VINEGAR)

Stir together the cooking wine, oyster sauce, shrimp paste, soy sauce, garlic, peppercorns, ginger, star anise, chile paste, fermented black beans, dry mustard, peanut oil, and vinegar in a saucepan set over low heat. Simmer as gently as possible for 10 to 12 minutes. Remove the sauce from the heat and let it sit for at least 1 hour at room temperature to allow the flavors to blend (or let it sit for as long as it takes to cook the pork).

— SAMBAL MAYONNAISE —

This is a magical combination, which is great on everything from this sandwich to roast vegetables to fish. Spread it around.

¼ CUP/60 ML SAMBAL OELEK

½ CUP/120 ML MAYONNAISE (FULL FAT!)

In a small bowl, combine the sambal oelek and mayonnaise. Stir and refrigerate for up to 1 week if not using right away.

— PICKLED ONIONS —

The coriander seed is crucial to this bright, versatile condiment.
See if you don't agree—eggs, steak, chicken, and, most of all,
pork take to it gleefully.

1 LARGE ONION, PREFERABLY VIDALIA,
VERY THINLY SLICED

1/2 CUP/120 ML CIDER VINEGAR

1/2 CUP/120 ML WATER

1 TBSP CORIANDER SEED, COARSELY CRUSHED

1/4 TSP GROUND TURMERIC

Place the onion in an extra-large cereal bowl. Combine the vinegar,
water, coriander seed, and turmeric in a small saucepan set over
high heat and bring to a boil. Remove from the heat and pour over
the onion. Allow the onion to sit for 1 hour at room temperature.
Store, refrigerated, for up to 10 days.

THICK-CUT CHOPS WITH PEANUT MASALA,
CILANTRO RAITA, AND
SPICY RED LENTILS

SERVES 4

When I made this spice-loaded peanut masala for the first time, I couldn't get it out of my head. The morning after our meal, I sought out the remnant and ate it alongside the lentils I frequently breakfast on. The layers of toasted spices, combined with the richness of ground peanuts, makes an extraordinarily intense condiment.

— THICK-CUT CHOPS WITH PEANUT MASALA —

FOUR 12-OZ/340-G BONE-IN THICK-CUT CHOPS

1 TSP ORGANIC HIGH-HEAT OIL, PLUS 1 TBSP (SEE HIGH-TEMPERATURE COOKING OILS, PAGE 17)

1½ TSP KOSHER SALT

½ CUP/70 G ROASTED SALTED PEANUTS

10 DRIED PEQUIN CHILES (SUBSTITUTE FRESH OR DRIED SERRANOS, OR 1 HABAÑERO)

1 TBSP CUMIN SEED

2 TBSP CORIANDER SEED

1 TSP GREEN PEPPERCORNS

1 TSP *CHARNUSHKA* (ALSO CALLED NIGELLA SEEDS, OPTIONAL)

1 TBSP COCONUT FAT (SUBSTITUTE BUTTER)

2 LARGE GARLIC CLOVES

Preheat the oven to 300°F/150°C. (To grill, see the instructions on page 126.) Dry the chops all over, coat with the 1 tsp oil and ½ tsp of the salt, and set on the counter for 30 minutes to 1 hour to take the chill off.

Combine the remaining 1 tsp salt, the peanuts, chiles, cumin seed, coriander seed, green peppercorns, and *charnushka* (if using) in a food processor and process for 1 to 2 minutes, or until the mixture is the texture of fine bread crumbs. Heat the coconut fat in a sauté pan set over low heat. Add the spice mixture and toast for 1 to 2 minutes, stirring frequently. (If the mixture begins to smoke, take it off the heat and stir vigorously.) Once it's hot and fragrant, remove from the heat and add the garlic, stirring to keep the garlic from burning. Set the hot pan aside to allow the garlic to gently finish cooking in the heat of the spices.

Heat a large cast-iron pan over high heat, add the remaining 1 tbsp oil and, when it shimmers, carefully place the chops in the pan. Cook for 3 to 5 minutes on the first side and 2 to 3 on the second to brown the exterior. Set in the oven, pan and all, for 5 to 10 minutes, or until the internal temperature of the thickest chop reaches 145°F/63°C on an instant-read thermometer. (Thick-cut 1½-in/4-cm chops may take another 5 minutes or so.) The meat is done when it's pink, but not bloody, and the texture is slightly granular, not slippery and smooth as it is when raw.

Transfer the chops to a warm plate and coat generously on both sides with a layer of the reserved peanut masala (some of it will fall off onto the plate). Pass any remaining masala at the table.

— CILANTRO RAITA —

Raita is a fine, cooling condiment. Greek yogurt contains more milk solids than American-style yogurt and will result in a richer-tasting, thicker sauce. It's everywhere these days; look for a brand, such as Fage, that contains nothing more than milk and active yogurt cultures.

1 CUCUMBER, PEELED AND DICED

½ TSP KOSHER SALT

1 CUP/240 ML FULL-FAT PLAIN GREEK YOGURT

1 CUP/40 G FRESH CILANTRO LEAVES

½ CUP/20 G COARSELY CHOPPED FRESH MINT LEAVES

Toss the cucumber and salt together in a bowl and set aside for at least 15 minutes. Spread out an immaculate dish towel or a piece of cheesecloth and place the cucumber in the center (leave any liquid behind). Wrap it up in a bundle and squeeze to extract the remaining liquid.

Combine the cucumber, yogurt, cilantro, and mint in a food processor or blender and work for 30 seconds, or until you have green yogurt with flecks of leaf. Transfer to a bowl and serve.

— SPICY RED LENTILS —

Spicy, fragrant legumes are one of my favorite foods. Use any kind of lentil—the cooking time will vary, so check frequently and begin with a little less water, adding more as needed until the lentils are tender, but not mushy.

2 TBSP BUTTER OR COCONUT FAT

1 RED ONION, HALVED AND THINLY SLICED

¼ TSP GROUND TURMERIC

1 TSP MADRAS CURRY POWDER

1 TSP CELERY SEED

1 TSP CUMIN SEED

1 BLACK CARDAMOM POD

3 DRIED PEQUIN CHILES OR ANOTHER DRIED OR FRESH HOT CHILE, WITH SEEDS, CHOPPED

3¼ CUPS/780 ML WATER

4 CUPS/455 G RED LENTILS, RINSED AND DRAINED

1½ TSP KOSHER SALT

In a large saucepan with a lid, melt the butter over low heat. Add the onion, stir to coat, and add the turmeric, curry powder, celery seed, cumin seed, cardamom pod, and chiles. Stir and cook for 1 to 2 minutes. When the spices begin to stick to the pot, add ¼ cup/60 ml of the water. Cook, stirring frequently, for another 8 to 10 minutes, until the onion is soft and the water has evaporated. Stir in the remaining 3 cups/720 ml water and the lentils, cover, and cook over low heat for 8 to 10 minutes. Turn off the heat, add the salt, stir gently, and cover the pot. Set aside for 5 minutes. The lentils should still have some shape, but they should be tender. Transfer to a bowl and serve.

PAN-FRIED CHOPS
WITH PEANUT SAUCE, CUCUMBER-WATERMELON SALAD, AND STICKY RICE

SERVES 4

I would happily eat peanut sauce for breakfast, but then I eat my steel-cut oats in the morning with Sriracha sauce, maple syrup, and coarse salt, so maybe I'm not the best example. Peanuts and pork are, in any case, an intuitive combination. This is a summer meal, given the refreshing Cucumber-Watermelon Salad, but in winter you could simply swap the salad out for Spicy Red Lentils (page 205) or for Roasted Yams and Maitake Mushrooms (page 175). Sticky rice is, of course, irresistible in any season—and the perfect food for toddlers who haven't yet mastered the art of cutlery.

— PAN-FRIED CHOPS —

FOUR 12- TO 14-OZ/ 340- TO 400-G BONE-IN LOIN CHOPS, 1½ IN/4 CM THICK

1 TSP KOSHER SALT

2 TBSP ORGANIC HIGH-HEAT OIL (SEE HIGH-TEMPERATURE COOKING OILS, PAGE 17)

PEANUT SAUCE (RECIPE FOLLOWS)

4 GREEN ONIONS, TRIMMED TOP AND BOTTOM AND THINLY SLICED (USE IT ALL)

¼ CUP/35 G CHOPPED ROASTED SALTED PEANUTS

FLAKY SALT AND BLACK PEPPER FOR FINISHING

Preheat the oven to 300°F/150°C. Dry the chops, sprinkle them with the kosher salt, and set them out to rest on the counter for 30 minutes to 1 hour to take the chill off.

Heat a large cast-iron pan over high heat until very hot. Add the oil and cook the chops on the first side until browned, 5 minutes. Turn over and cook for 3 to 5 minutes on the second side (you'll have some smoke in the air by now). When the second side is browned, set the pan in the oven and let the meat roast gently for 12 to 15 minutes, or until an instant-read thermometer inserted into the thickest part of a chop reads 145°F/63°C. The meat is done when it's pink, but not bloody, and the texture is slightly granular, not slippery and smooth as it is when raw.

Take the pan out of the oven, place the chops on a plate, and spread a little peanut sauce over the surface of each chop. Finish with a scattering of green onions and peanuts. Sprinkle with flaky salt and a few grinds of pepper. Pass the remaining sauce at the table when serving.

— PEANUT SAUCE —

Versatile and unfailingly tasty, this sauce can go on any pork as is; with a little more water, it can dress a noodle salad.

¼ CUP/60 G NATURAL SALTED PEANUT BUTTER

1 TBSP SOY SAUCE

2 TSP TOASTED SESAME OIL

1 TSP BROWN SUGAR (DARK OR LIGHT)

1 GARLIC CLOVE, MINCED

1 TBSP SAMBAL OELEK (HOT SAUCE WORKS, TOO)

¼ CUP/60 ML WATER

Combine the peanut butter, soy sauce, sesame oil, brown sugar, garlic, sambal oelek, and water in a small saucepan. Mix thoroughly, and when you're ready to use the sauce, heat gently until just hot. This keeps for 3 days at most.

— CUCUMBER-WATERMELON SALAD —

This is a crazy-good combination that's difficult to get enough of. It's so refreshing and pretty, you'll find yourself making it again and again to combat the heat of summer. If you omit the watermelon, add cooked noodles, and toss with thinned peanut sauce, you'll have a stand-alone lunch.

1 ENGLISH (SEEDLESS) CUCUMBER, DICED

1 LB/455 G WATERMELON, SEEDED AND DICED

1 TBSP RICE VINEGAR

1 TBSP BEST OLIVE OIL (SEE OLIVE OIL, PAGE 18)

¼ CUP/10 G CHOPPED FRESH MINT

BLACK PEPPER

FLAKY SALT

In a serving bowl, combine the cucumber, watermelon, vinegar, olive oil, mint, and a grind of black pepper. Add the salt to the surface of the salad just before serving. Be sure the salad is cold when it goes to the table!

— STICKY RICE —

Most recipes for sticky rice call for steaming the rice in a bamboo basket steamer or a metal steamer lined with cheesecloth. I've made sticky rice in a pot the same way I make regular rice, but steaming gives a more a translucent grain and will ensure you don't scald the rice on the bottom of the pan.

2 CUPS/380 G STICKY OR SWEET RICE (ALSO CALLED GLUTINOUS RICE)

4 CUPS/960 ML WATER

1 TBSP RICE VINEGAR

2 TSP MIRIN

6 GREEN ONIONS, TRIMMED TOP AND BOTTOM AND THINLY SLICED (USE IT ALL)

Combine the rice and water in a large saucepan and soak for at least 1 hour or overnight. Drain the rice, but do not rinse. Use a length of cheesecloth to line a steamer basket or colander that fits into one of your pots with a tight-fitting lid. Fill the pot with water, and put the rice in the steamer basket. Cook, covered, over medium-low heat for 15 to 20 minutes, or until the rice is tender and the water is absorbed. Transfer to a serving bowl and stir in the rice vinegar and mirin. Sprinkle with the green onions and serve.

LEMONGRASS CHOPS
WITH MIXED PICKLES AND PEANUT-COCONUT SLAW

SERVES 4

These chops are inspired by the thin, charred chops so frequently on the menu at Thai restaurants. Making them at home with terrific pork means they're redolent with the magical essence of lemongrass, genus *Cymbopogon*, which includes more than fifty varieties native to India and the Asian tropics. A regular show stealer in many a recipe, you'll find full contact here. The Peanut-Coconut Slaw is this pork's perfect match, with pickles for a kick of acid.

— LEMONGRASS CHOPS —

⅓ CUP/35 G THIN ROUNDS OF LEMONGRASS

2 TBSP ORGANIC HIGH-HEAT OIL (SEE HIGH-TEMPERATURE COOKING OILS, PAGE 17)

¼ CUP/60 ML FISH SAUCE

1 SERRANO OR JALAPEÑO CHILE

2 TBSP DARK SOY SAUCE
(I LIKE DARK MUSHROOM SOY)

1 TBSP DARK BROWN SUGAR

2½ TO 3 LB/1.2 TO 1.4 KG THIN-CUT BLADE OR RIB-END CHOPS

½ CUP/20 G CHOPPED FRESH THAI BASIL (SUBSTITUTE A COMBINATION OF FRESH MINT AND ITALIAN BASIL)

Combine the lemongrass, oil, fish sauce, chile, soy sauce, and brown sugar in a blender and work until smooth. Pour the marinade into a large mixing bowl (or a large ziplock bag) and add the chops. Move the chops around to coat on all sides and marinate for 1 hour on the counter, or, better yet, overnight in the refrigerator. (Let the chops rest at room temperature for 30 minutes before cooking if you do marinate in the refrigerator.)

Build a medium fire in a charcoal or wood grill or heat a gas grill to medium. If you're using charcoal or wood, you want hot embers, not flames. Use a clean, well-cured grate.

Grill the chops over direct heat for 5 to 8 minutes a side, depending on the intensity of your fire, turning frequently to avoid flare-ups. The meat should be quite dark, almost charred. If your chops are thin, they will be completely cooked once they're browned on both sides. Transfer to a plate and place in a warming oven for 5 minutes. Sprinkle the chops with basil and serve.

— MIXED PICKLES —

Pickles are all the rage these days. Don't even try escaping every arty variety if you live within three states of hipster Brooklyn, New York. This is a snarky way of saying there are great pickles to buy these days, but just because you can buy greatness doesn't mean you can't choose to make your own. Like the Sesame Broccoli (page 167), these are inspired by my friend Kazumi Futagawa, who clued me into the brilliance of adding bonito flakes, plum purée, and mirin to the pickle brine. They are more Japanese than Thai, and I've added a hint of lemongrass to really confuse things. I like to think of the word "mixed" here as having more than one meaning. Add a hard-boiled egg or other vegetables to the brine as you wish. I like baby green beans, okra, and beets. (It's best to make a separate jar of pickled beets using this brine, since the color will spoil the appearance of the other vegetables.)

1 CUP/240 ML WATER

HEAPING 1 TBSP FUERU WAKAME THREADS
(DRIED SEAWEED)

HEAPING 1 TBSP BONITO FLAKES

ONE 3-IN/7.5-CM PIECE FRESH GINGER, PEELED,
CUT INTO 5 ROUNDS, AND CRUSHED

HEAPING 1 TSP PICKLED PLUM PURÉE
(UMEBOSHI PASTE)

3 TBSP MIRIN

1/2 CARROT, PEELED AND JULIENNED
(CUT INTO MATCHSTICKS)

ONE 6-IN/15-CM DAIKON, PEELED AND JULIENNED

1 ASIAN CUCUMBER OR 2 KIRBY CUCUMBERS,
CUT INTO ROUNDS ABOUT 1/2 IN/12 MM THICK

1 STALK LEMONGRASS, CUT INTO THIN ROUNDS
(TENDER PART ONLY)

1 1/4 TO 1 1/2 CUPS/300 TO 360 ML RICE VINEGAR

In a small saucepan set over medium heat, combine the water, wakame threads, and bonito flakes. Heat until the mixture just begins to simmer, then turn off the heat. Stir in the ginger, plum purée, and mirin. Pack the carrot, daikon, cucumber, and lemongrass into a 1-qt/960-ml canning jar, and pour the hot liquid and all the solids in the pan over them. Top with the rice vinegar, filling the jar nearly to the rim. Let the vegetables macerate at room temperature for at least 1 hour before eating. They will keep, tightly covered, in the refrigerator for at least 3 weeks, and you can add vegetables to the existing brine as you munch your way through the contents of the jar.

— PEANUT-COCONUT SLAW —

The trick to this stunning, tropically inflected slaw is coconut oil. Fragrant and glossy, the whole achieves that pinnacle of balance between sweet and salty, which is something of a receding horizon when it comes to slaw. Most Asian recipes call for raw, unsalted peanuts, but they're so difficult to find I often end up using roasted salted peanuts. If you have raw peanuts, toast them in a pan and give them a sprinkling of salt (see On Toasting Seeds, Nuts, and Spices on page 18).

1 SMALL HEAD SAVOY CABBAGE, CORED AND CHOPPED

2 TBSP HONEY

1/4 CUP/60 ML VIRGIN COCONUT OIL

1/2 TSP KOSHER SALT

1/4 CUP/60 ML RICE VINEGAR

GRATED ZEST OF 2 LIMES

1/2 CUP/70 G CHOPPED ROASTED SALTED PEANUTS

FLAKY SALT (OPTIONAL)

Place the cabbage in a large mixing bowl. Heat the honey, coconut oil, kosher salt, and vinegar in a small saucepan set over low heat until the honey dissolves into the coconut oil. Allow to cool briefly and then stir in the lime zest and pour over the cabbage. Add the peanuts and toss thoroughly. Taste and add a little flaky salt (or more vinegar), as you wish before serving.

SAMBAL BUTTER-STUFFED TENDERLOIN
WITH PERSIMMON SAUCE, BLACKENED BABY PEPPERS, AND MINTED RICE SQUARES

SERVES 4

Sambal butter is a bit like sambal mayonnaise—the combination of one plus one does not equal two. Something about mixing chile garlic paste (*sambal oelek*) with fat transforms the simple ingredients, Rumpelstiltskin-like, from straw into gold. This butter effortlessly corrects the greatest sin of tenderloin, its leanness, while imparting great flavor and a little heat. Add the Persimmon Sauce for a tart, fruity note, placed in proximity to the Blackened Baby Peppers and fragrant Minted Rice Squares, for, as the saying goes, "the best results."

— SAMBAL BUTTER-STUFFED TENDERLOIN —

ONE 1-LB/455-G TENDERLOIN

1/2 TSP KOSHER SALT

4 TBSP/55 G BUTTER, AT ROOM TEMPERATURE

1 SMALL SHALLOT, MINCED

2 TBSP SAMBAL OELEK

2 TBSP ORGANIC HIGH-HEAT OIL
(SEE HIGH-TEMPERATURE COOKING OILS, PAGE 17)

Dry the meat and cut it deeply down the center lengthwise, without cutting all the way through into two pieces. Salt the meat inside and out and set aside on the counter. In a small bowl combine the butter, shallot, and sambal oelek. Mash with a fork until all the ingredients are thoroughly integrated.

Distribute about two-thirds of the sambal butter along the length of the cut sides of the meat. Pinch the two attached halves together, pressing the butter back into the meat. Cut a 5- to 6-ft/1.5- to 1.8-m length of butcher's string and tie a knot around one end so that it holds the cut closed. Wrap the string around the meat four or five times to reach the other end. Switch back, making a crisscross pattern with the string. Tie the remaining end to the loose end of the initial knot.

Preheat the oven to 300°F/150°C. Heat the oil over high heat in a large frying pan, preferably cast-iron. Place the meat, cut-side up, in the hot oil and cook until the bottom browns up nicely, 5 to 8 minutes. Transfer the meat, pan and all, to the oven and roast for 15 to 20 minutes, or until the meat firms up slightly, giving only lightly when poked. The internal temperature should be about 140°F/60°C. Remove the meat from the oven and let it rest for 5 minutes before slicing (it will gain several degrees as it rests) and serving.

— PERSIMMON SAUCE —

Persimmons are vastly underappreciated, given how tasty, pretty, and versatile they are. To make this sauce, you'll need to find (or wait for) Hachiya persimmons that feel like jelly beneath the skin when you squeeze them. Trust me, they're not overripe—they're perfect. When firm, the fruit is as unpleasantly tannic and astringent as anything I've tasted. Do not substitute Fuyu persimmons here—they're great for salads but aren't the right consistency for this sauce, unless you purée them.

2 VERY RIPE HACHIYA PERSIMMONS, PEELED AND MASHED

2 TBSP RICE VINEGAR

HEAPING 2 TBSP PICKLED JAPANESE GINGER, COARSELY CHOPPED

Combine the persimmons, rice vinegar, and pickled ginger in a small saucepan. Set the mixture over very low heat and bring it just to a simmer. Remove from the heat and serve hot.

— BLACKENED BABY PEPPERS —

More and more frequently, I find loose or bagged multicolored baby
sweet peppers at the grocery store. They're pretty, easy to cook,
and never fail to tempt when they're roasted to sweet submission
in a very hot oven and tossed with oil, coarse salt, and a
drop of vinegar.

1½ LB/680 G SMALL SWEET PEPPERS (PREFERABLY
A MIX OF ORANGE, RED, AND YELLOW)

2 TBSP PEANUT OR VEGETABLE OIL

½ TSP KOSHER SALT

½ TSP RICE VINEGAR

FLAKY SALT FOR FINISHING

Preheat the oven to 500°F/260°C. In a large mixing bowl, toss together
the peppers, peanut oil, and kosher salt. Lay out the peppers on a
baking sheet (lined with parchment if you like) and roast for 12 to
15 minutes, or until blackened on the bottom and sides. Transfer the
whole peppers to a serving bowl and toss with the vinegar. Add a
pinch of flaky salt and serve.

— MINTED RICE SQUARES —

These little squares are pretty and easy to make. Rather than a
scoop of rice, you have a neat little square, redolent with coconut
and mint. (If you can't be bothered with the squares, the rice is
pretty great served loose.)

1½ CUPS/285 G JASMINE RICE,
RINSED AND DRAINED

2 CUPS/480 ML UNSWEETENED COCONUT MILK

1 CUP/240 ML WATER

1 TSP KOSHER SALT

¼ CUP/10 G CHOPPED FRESH MINT

Line a 6-by-12-in/15-by-30.5-cm baking sheet with parchment paper. In
a medium saucepan with a tight-fitting lid, combine the rice, coconut
milk, water, and salt. Cover and set over medium heat for 12 to
15 minutes, or until the liquid has been absorbed by the rice. Mix
in the mint. Press the rice onto the prepared baking sheet and
refrigerate for about 1 hour to set. Before serving, preheat the
oven to 200°F/95°C and put the rice in the oven for 5 to 7 minutes,
or until just hot. Cut into neat squares and serve.

SMOKED BABY BACK RIBS, JASMINE RICE WITH ASIAN GREENS AND SHIITAKES, AND GREEN PAPAYA-CRISPY PORK BELLY SALAD

SERVES 4

Soy sauce, green onions, and pork go extremely well with hardwood smoke. Making ribs is not difficult, so don't be cowed by all the hype about doing it right. Just buy the best meat you can afford along with some lump hardwood charcoal and go at it. You will need 2 or 3 handfuls hardwood chips, soaked in water for 30 minutes or more and drained, for smoking the meat.

— SMOKED BABY BACK RIBS —

4 TO 5 LB/1.4 TO 2.3 KG BABY BACK RIBS
(2 OR 3 SLABS), SILVERSKIN REMOVED
(SEE THE INSTRUCTIONS ON PAGE 15)

1 TSP KOSHER SALT

BLACK PEPPER

¼ CUP/60 ML DARK SOY SAUCE
(MUSHROOM IF YOU HAVE IT)

1 TBSP SAMBAL OELEK

6 TO 8 GREEN ONIONS, TRIMMED TOP AND BOTTOM
AND THINLY SLICED (USE IT ALL)

Place the ribs in a large, flat baking dish (such as a glass casserole dish), and coat them with the salt, a grind of pepper, the soy sauce, and sambal oelek. Set to marinate if you have time (up to 24 hours in the refrigerator) or bring them right to the grill. (If you refrigerate, allow them to rest for 30 minutes on the counter to take the chill off before grilling.)

Build a medium fire in a charcoal or wood grill or heat a gas grill to medium. If you're using charcoal or wood, you want hot embers, not flames. (If you don't have a grill large enough to place the meat away from the heat source, make a small fire or set the grill to its lowest setting.) Use a clean, well-cured grate. Place a handful of wood chips on the fire. Repeat every hour, adding charcoal or wood and wood chips to maintain the smoke and a steady temperature. Add fuel more frequently if the temperature dips below 200°F/95°C. It should hover between 200 and 350°F/95 and 180°C.

Place the ribs a few inches/centimetres away from the heat source if possible. Cover the grill, and smoke for 3 to 3½ hours. Baby back ribs, depending on how big and fatty they are, can dry out, so watch and check frequently. Every hour, flip the meat over. The ribs are done when you can easily pull a bone off the rack and the exterior is a delicious crusty brown. Transfer the ribs to a platter, cut them into sections, and serve scattered with the green onions.

— JASMINE RICE WITH ASIAN GREENS — AND SHIITAKES

The shiitakes in this recipe deliver their big, smoky flavor and a wonderfully chewy, spongy texture to rice tossed with lightly cooked greens. Fish sauce and the smallest hint of spice bring the three elements together.

1 TBSP PEANUT OR VEGETABLE OIL

8 OZ/225 G SHIITAKE MUSHROOMS, STEMMED AND THINLY SLICED

¼ TSP KOSHER SALT

4 SMALL HEADS BOK CHOY, OR 1 LARGE BUNCH MUSTARD GREENS OR KALE, CUT INTO RIBBONS (ANY COMBINATION IS FINE, TOO)

1 TBSP FISH SAUCE

1 TBSP SAMBAL OELEK

1 TBSP RICE VINEGAR

2 CUPS/200 G COOKED JASMINE RICE (PAGE 185)

Heat the peanut oil in a large sauté pan over medium-high heat. Add the shiitakes and salt and cook, stirring frequently, for 2 to 3 minutes, or until the shiitakes have shrunk and are fragrant. Add the greens, fish sauce, and sambal oelek and cook for another 2 to 3 minutes, or until the greens are just tender. Mix in the vinegar thoroughly, add the rice, and toss. Serve hot.

— GREEN PAPAYA–CRISPY PORK BELLY SALAD —

The brilliance of combining pork belly, fish sauce, and papaya is
unsurpassed. Keep an icy beer handy to slug as you gobble up this
spicy, seductive salad. Make plenty.

1 LB/455 G SLOW-COOKED PORK BELLY
(PAGE 67), CUT INTO 1/2-IN/12-MM CUBES

1 MEDIUM HEAD GREEN CABBAGE,
CORED AND THINLY SLICED

1/3 CUP/80 ML FISH SAUCE

1/4 CUP/60 ML ORGANIC REFINED OLIVE OIL
(SEE OLIVE OIL, PAGE 18)

1/4 CUP/60 ML RICE VINEGAR

1 CUP/140 G COARSELY CHOPPED ROASTED
SALTED PEANUTS

3 TBSP SHRIMP PASTE WITH SOYBEAN OIL

1 OR 2 THAI CHILES, MINCED (SUBSTITUTE
A HABAÑERO, SERRANO, OR JALAPEÑO)

1 MEDIUM GREEN PAPAYA, CUBED

1/2 CUP/50 G UNSWEETENED COCONUT FLAKES,
TOASTED (SEE ON TOASTING NUTS, SEEDS,
AND SPICES, PAGE 18)

COARSE OR FLAKY SALT

SRIRACHA SAUCE OR CAYENNE PEPPER,
AS NEEDED (OPTIONAL)

Preheat the oven to 250°F/120°C. Spread out the pork belly on a
baking sheet and cook for about 15 minutes, or until crispy and
the fat begins to render. Remove from the oven and set aside.

In a large bowl, combine the cabbage, fish sauce, olive oil, vinegar,
peanuts, shrimp paste, chiles, papaya, coconut flakes, and pork belly.
Toss together thoroughly, add a pinch of salt, and taste. Adjust for
spice (add more chiles, a squirt of Sriracha, or a pinch of cayenne)
and salt before serving.

INDEX